This book is about qu
that—it is a book about ans
tions from people who were not always honest seekers. How Jesus
"answers" his critics contains lessons for us all, which Mink explores
with a reader's wonder and a pastor's heart. Believers and non-believers will both benefit from this book, with one proviso—that they honestly seek the One who is the way, the truth, and the life. Thoughtful
and probing questions at the conclusion of each chapter make this
book especially ideal for church groups and small-group Bible studies.

David L. Matson, Ph.D.

Professor of Biblical Studies

Hope International University

In his book Questioning Jesus: Considering His Responses Bob
Mink brings the life of Jesus to a brighter light. In it we get snapshots
of how Jesus handled his critics. Helping us first understand the setting of these accounts of Jesus being questioned, Bob then sheds light
on how we can apply Jesus' responses to our lives. This is an engaging
resource for individual inspiration or group Bible study.

Bryan Sands

Director of Campus Ministries

Hope International University

"There is a difference between asking someone questions and
questioning someone." How true the opening sentence of this book
is. I think we can all tell when someone is asking us a question and
when we're being questioned; how much more so for Jesus! Who has
the nerve to question Jesus? Well, actually, I think we all have; I know
I have. In this provocative book Bob Mink looks at a number of stories
in the life of Jesus where He is questioned. Read and discuss how Jesus
answered those questions and those who asked them. Learn more

about Jesus and learn more about yourself. This book will most certainly make you think.

Randy Paredes, Lead Pastor
Florence Christian Church

Often the best answer to a question is a question. Jesus was a master of this approach to teaching and learning. Bob Mink masterfully conveys Jesus' responses to those questioning Him. This book will help answer your questions about Jesus by causing you to find your answers through questions.

Dr. Joseph C. Grana II
Dean of Pacific College of Ministry and Biblical Studies
Hope International University

I wholeheartedly recommend this book to any individual or Bible Study Group. Bob Mink's perspective on the verbal challenges Jesus faced from his detractors is unique and thought-provoking. His abilities as an insightful Bible teacher shine through; his in-depth scripture analysis gives the reader excellent food for thought on each chapter's "questioning" topic. I have long admired his ability to communicate the written word. I look forward to reading more offerings from him in (what I hope are) future books.

Dennis Trimble,
Elder and Bible Study Leader
Discovery Christian Church

Bob Mink brings his 40 plus years of teaching/preaching experience to the written page and continues to demonstrate an uncanny ability to challenge, encourage, and spur believers on to personal growth. This book is an excellent tool for individual reflection or group and discussion. He challenges the reader to think about his or her own convictions, faith walk, and beliefs about who Jesus is and was and what Jesus means to them on a personal level. The discussion questions at the end of each chapter are thought provoking and cause one to reflect and dig deep.

Diane Ewing,
Former Director of Women's Ministry
Discovery Christian Church

This study is a unique look into the character of Jesus as He responds to questions asked during His ministry. Pastor Mink skillfully focuses on the questioners, the reason for the question and Jesus' response, as well as his own analysis of the situation. This study would make a valuable contribution to anyone caring to study the life of Jesus, His humanity and divinity, in addition to the impact He made during His ministry. A perfect individual or group study text!

Mike Kelley,
Bible Study Leader and Former Elder
Discovery Christian Church

Questioning Jesus

By Bob Mink

Bob Mink
14766 Rio Grande Dr.
Moreno Valley, CA 92556

Book Layout © 2014 BookDesignTemplates.com

Questioning Jesus/Bob Mink – 1ˢᵗ Edition
ISBN-13: 978-1517785857
ISBN-10: 1517785855

DEDICATION

To all those who have participated in Bible studies I have led and classes I have taught in the churches and schools I have had the privilege of serving.

JESUS, THIS IS YOU

Rich in mercy, full of grace
Endless worship to Your name
God of power, kindness, righteousness
It is You; Jesus, this is You

Jesus, You are greater than the grave
Jesus, You have broken every chain
Forever You will reign
Forever we will sing
Jesus, this is You

Deep in wisdom, perfect peace
Author, master, majesty
God of power, kindness, righteousness
It is You; Jesus, this is You
It is You; Jesus, this is You

Hallelujah to the One who is able
Hallelujah! Our God, Jesus, this is You
Hallelujah! Praise the One who is faithful
Hallelujah! Our God, Jesus, this is You

Jesus, You are greater than the grave
Jesus, You have broken every chain
Forever You will reign
Forever we will sing
Jesus, this is You
This is You
Jesus, this is You

TABLE OF CONTENTS

ACKNOWLEDGEMENTS

I want to thank Jennifer Johnson for her excellent work in editing this manuscript and for writing such a thoughtful foreword. Thanks also to Joe Grana, Dean of Pacific Christian College of Ministry and Biblical Studies, for the opportunity to teach at Hope International University.

FOREWORD

I've never met Bob Mink.

When I was growing up I heard my dad mention his name. A few times they spoke at the same conference or worked together on the same project, and I knew dad liked Bob and appreciated his ministry. I had never met Bob, but he seemed like a good man.

Fast forward several years to 2014 when Bob asked me to edit his first book, a memoir of his four decades as a minister featuring some of the letters he'd sent and received over the years. For months we worked together as he entrusted me with this manuscript so close to his heart. For months I read, edited, and formatted the words that summarized his significant ministry. For months I was impressed by his candor and his honesty as he included not only notes from people who affirmed or complimented him, but also some from those who challenged or confronted him. As I read the words he wrote to his church, his children, and his colleagues, I agreed with my dad. I had never met Bob, but this was a good man.

This week Bob complimented me by asking me to write this foreword. Questioning Jesus is the second book we've worked on together, and once again I am concluding the work with an appreciation for him and for his gifts. Concisely but thoroughly, Bob addresses many of the questions people asked Jesus during his brief earthly ministry, explores Jesus' responses, and offers helpful historical and theological context. Bob is a scholar as well as a pastor, and his ability to combine the two makes this book accessible to someone starting a faith journey as well as a seasoned saint looking for new insight.

I still have not met Bob in person, but through his words and through our work I know him—and I know Jesus better, too. My prayer is that you will grow in your own faith as you read Bob's insights in this book.

Jennifer Johnson
December 2015

INTRODUCTION

There is a difference between asking someone questions and questioning someone. When we ask people questions it is with the goal of getting information. But when we question someone it implies we think they are wrong, they don't know what they're talking about, or they are not being totally truthful.

While the title of this book does describe what it is about, it is also intentionally provocative. The idea of "questioning Jesus" is no doubt unsettling for committed Christians. Those of us who believe He is the Son of God and our Savior and Lord find it disturbing. And yet people question Jesus all the time. You may have questioned Him yourself.

Some question Jesus in terms of the historical accuracy of the biblical record of His life, words, and deeds. Did He do and say the things the four Gospels of Matthew, Mark, Luke, and John report? Did Jesus really heal people, calm a storm, walk on water, raise people from the dead, and come back to life after His crucifixion?

There are questions raised about other parts of the Bible, as well. In view of what many consider overwhelming evidence for evolution, how can we believe in biblical creation? Or how can followers of Jesus justify the killing carried out by the people of God in the Old Testament? Is homosexuality really a sin?

Others question Jesus from a philosophical perspective. Often phrased as "the problem of evil," people wonder why God allows suffering. Does Jesus care about my pain? Why does He allow children to be abused and wars to be fought? If God is good, why does He permit evil?

One of the most unsettling lines of questioning to me personally concerns the conduct of Christians. Why don't those who claim to be committed to Jesus live more like Him? Why is the church at large so fragmented? Why do some who claim Jesus as Lord seem to despise others who make the same claim?

The specific field of Christian study that deals with questions like these is called apologetics. The goal of apologetics is to establish the reasonableness of the Christian faith and provide responses to questions and attacks including the above examples.[1] Apologetics, however, is not the purpose or focus of this book. Bible study is; or, more specifically, the purpose is the study of selected parts of the Gospels.

Questioning Jesus is nothing new. The Bible tells us about many times Jesus was questioned during His ministry. There were times when people asked Jesus "honest" questions seeking information, but that wasn't always the case; often Jesus' critics questioned Him as a way to tempt, test, discredit, trap, and delegitimize Him.

Something I found interesting in considering Jesus' responses in these accounts was the number of times Jesus responded with a question of His own. In nine of the thirteen occasions explored in the chapters that follow, Jesus asked His questioners a question. But Jesus' questions had a different purpose than theirs. He was not interested in arguing, but instead challenging His questioners to think.

The issues raised in these exchanges tell us a lot about those who questioned Jesus. But more importantly, Jesus' responses tell us about Him. Those who witnessed the back and forth were impressed and we are still impressed today as we read the accounts.

In biblical and theological studies, the area of study focusing on Jesus is called Christology. My first class on the subject many years ago was entitled "The Person and Work of Christ." Briefly stated, Christology is the study of who Jesus was and what He did. But for those of us who are Christians, it is more than just who Jesus was and what He did. Because of our faith in Him we are equally interested in who Jesus still is and what He still does.

To learn all we can about who Jesus was and is and what He did and does, we would need to consider everything the Gospels tell us about Him as well as the teaching about Him in the rest of the New Testament. But that could fill many books! My focus in this book is exploring a variety of scenes in the Gospels where Jesus was questioned. If we pay attention to these encounters and the way Jesus responded, we can learn a great deal about Him.

CHAPTER ONE

What Kind of Messiah Will You Be?

Primary Bible References – Matthew 4:1-11; Mark 1:9-13; and Luke 4:1-13

L ike me, I'm sure you've taken a lot of tests in your life. I don't remember any of the tests I took in grade school, but I know I had them. And, of course, we all had lots of them in middle school and high school. I remember one very important test I took in high school, one we all really wanted to pass: the test to get our driver's license. Later most of us took the SAT to get into college and then we faced dreaded "final exams" at the end of every semester or quarter. Some take personality tests in preparation for getting married. Every three months I get a blood test and once a year I get my eyes tested— neither of these requires preparation!

The New Testament Gospels tell us about a variety of ways Jesus was tested during His life and ministry. The tests He faced were unlike any of the examples listed above. These were tests to trick, trap, and discredit Him. Interestingly enough, the first test we read about in the Bible was not presented to Jesus by human beings, but by the devil. This test appears in both Matthew and Luke's Gospel.

Context and Setting

The context and setting in which Jesus was tested by Satan underscores the importance of the test. It came immediately following His baptism. And while Jesus' baptism was not the same as ours today, like ours, His was significant in terms of what it meant. Matthew, Mark, and Luke all tell us about Jesus' baptism with minor variations.

Matthew 3:14-15 tells us John was reluctant to baptize Jesus, but Jesus affirmed "it is proper for us to do this to fulfill all righteousness." John was correct in the sense that Jesus did not need to be baptized as an expression of repentance, but by His submission to baptism Jesus was identifying with those He came to save who did need to repent.

Matthew, Mark, and Luke all agree that at Jesus' baptism the Spirit of God descended on Him as a dove and God's voice was heard affirming Jesus as His Son and expressing His pleasure. Isn't it interesting that all three persons of the trinity are mentioned at Jesus' baptism? The Son, the Spirit, and the Father are all present.

We should also note that Jesus' baptism marked the beginning of His ministry. After his report of the baptism, but before the test, Luke notes "Jesus was about 30 years old when he began his ministry" (Luke 3:23). Jesus' baptism marked the transition from His private life we know little about to His public life we know quite a bit about. Following His baptism Jesus began the process of fulfilling the purpose of His coming to earth.

Finally, in terms of the context and setting for the test that was to follow, all three Gospels tell us Jesus was led by the Spirit into the wilderness; however, Luke adds Jesus was "full of the Holy Spirit"

(Luke 4:1). The fact that Jesus was led into the wilderness is significant because it was similar to the testing of the children of Israel in the wilderness when they had been led out of Egyptian slavery under the leadership of Moses. But unlike the children of Israel who failed the wilderness tests, Jesus passed His tests.

Questioning Jesus and Considering His Responses

Mark reports simply that Jesus was tested by Satan, but both Matthew and Luke specify that the devil's questioning of Jesus was carried out with three specific tests. Bible students usually speak of this episode in terms of Jesus being tempted, and He was; but these temptations were also tests. The New International Version text reads "tempted" but also gives a footnote indicating "The Greek word for tempted can also mean tested." And in the editor's headings in the texts the words "tested" and "testing" are used.

Jesus was indeed tempted, but it was more than that. The devil began two of his temptations by questioning Jesus' identity with the phrase "if you are the Son of God" or, as it's sometimes rendered, "since you are the Son of God." As I suggest in the title of this chapter, in these tests the devil was challenging Jesus in terms of what kind of Messiah He would be. He gives two specific ways Jesus might prove who He was, both of which, along with the third temptation, challenged Jesus in terms of how He would carry out His mission on earth. How would He fulfill the purpose of His coming?

We do not know exactly how Satan tempted Jesus--whether he physically appeared to Jesus or presented himself and his challenges in some other way. If he indeed appeared to Jesus, his appearance was probably not anything like our traditional caricature of him. The

Apostle Paul does declare "Satan himself masquerades as an angel of light" (II Corinthians 11:14). All we know is that the devil questioned, tested, and tempted the Lord. And it is interesting to note that the only way we know about Jesus' being tested is that at some point He must have told His followers about it. New Testament scholar Bruce Metzger observes, "The story was remembered because of what it contributed to the early church's understanding of the significance of the person and work of Jesus."[2]

The First Test

The first test has the devil saying to Jesus, "If you are the Son of God, tell this stone to become bread" (Luke 4:3). What intensified this test was Jesus had fasted forty days and He was hungry. While others have fasted this long, a forty-day fast is certainly not common. And this was not a common situation; it was Jesus, the Son of God, at the outset of His mission.

We see in this temptation an indication of both the human as well as divine nature of Jesus. It was his human nature that wanted bread, but it was His divine nature that made it possible for Him to turn the stone into bread. I've never been tempted to turn stones to bread, have you? I've never been tempted because I can't do it. Jesus was tempted because He could have done it. But as paradoxical as it seems, not only Jesus' hunger, but the temptation to turn the stone into bread also confirms Jesus' true humanity. James 1:13 declares God cannot be tempted, so it was the human nature of Jesus that was tempted.

Jesus responded to this first test as He did to all three—by quoting Scripture. He cited Deuteronomy 8:3: "Man does not live on bread alone but on every word that comes from the mouth of the LORD."

This is what God had told His people through Moses when they were in the wilderness following the exodus from Egyptian slavery. And still today we do not live by bread alone. There is nothing wrong with bread—we need food in order to survive. As a matter of fact, there is nothing wrong with enjoying any of the physical things of life that God has given to us. There is nothing wrong with food, drink, recreation, rest, and sex. There's nothing wrong with being human; that's how God created us. It's the misuse of these gifts that is sin. But we must also remember that there is more to life than just the physical.

The questioning of Jesus in this first test was about more than just His identity as the Son of God. If Jesus was indeed the Son of God, would He use His divine power for His own advantage? We soon learn He wouldn't.

The Second Test

In his second test (in Luke's account) the devil promised Jesus all the authority and splendor of the world if He would simply worship him (Luke 4:5 and 6). The devil also told Jesus that it had been given to him and he could give it to anyone he wanted to. But was that true? Could the devil really deliver what he was promising? The answer is both yes and no. In John 12:31, looking to His saving death and subsequent resurrection, Jesus said, "Now is the time for judgment on this world; now the prince of this world will be driven out." We don't completely understand it, but God has allowed the devil to have considerable power. But whatever the devil can deliver is at best only temporary.

This second test the devil presented to Jesus was to see if He would compromise in order to gain status and power. In the end Jesus would have authority and splendor, but the path to that authority and splendor was not the easy one the devil presented to Him. God's plan was for Jesus to suffer and die. As He had done in response to the first temptation, Jesus again responded by quoting Scripture from Deuteronomy 6:13: "Worship the Lord your God and serve him only."

Some may believe this was a real test for Jesus, at least in terms of His human nature; but I cannot imagine that at this point Jesus considered this offer even for a moment. Much later near the end of His life, in the Garden before He was arrested, Jesus' prayer seems to suggest some struggle on His part. But Jesus stayed the course God had assigned to Him. And following His resurrection, before He returned to heaven, Jesus declared, "All authority in heaven and earth has been given to me" (Matthew 28:18). As a matter of fact, in the words of the Apostle Paul, "God exalted him to the highest place and gave him a name that is above every name" (Philippians 2:9). Jesus received what Satan offered not by compromising, but by carrying out His mission.

The Third Test

With the third test (in Luke's account) the devil took a cue from Jesus and cited a passage of Scripture himself. He challenged Jesus to jump off the temple and quoted Psalm 91:11-12, "He will command his angels concerning you to guard you carefully; they will lift you up in their hands, so that you will not strike your foot against a stone." Many Bible commentators see in this test the temptation for Jesus to win over followers by impressing them with God's power. After all, if Jesus jumped from the temple and was saved by angels it would be spectacular and garner a lot of attention.

Note that the devil can quote Scripture and he can also distort and misapply it. Jesus made that clear with His response of Deuteronomy 6:16: "Do not put the Lord your God to the test." And it isn't that God could not intervene in such situations. Remember Jesus' words to Peter when he used his sword the night Jesus was arrested. He instructed Peter to put his sword away and in Matthew 26:53 rhetorically asked him, "Do you think I cannot call on my Father, and he will at once put at my disposal more than twelve legions of angels?" To take the initiative in putting Himself in needless danger, in Jesus' view, would be to "put God to the test."

Wrap Up

So what can we learn from the devil's questioning of Jesus in this threefold test? In general terms we learn that Jesus was indeed the Son of God and He didn't need to prove it by taking Satan's bait. But we also learn that Jesus was fully human. Only if Jesus was truly human could He be tested by these temptations. We don't completely understand it, but Jesus was at the same time fully human and fully divine. Jesus Christ, the common name and designation for Him, suggests both aspects of His nature. Jesus is a human name and Christ (or Messiah) has a divine overtone.

Luke's conclusion to the account is important: "When the devil had finished all this tempting, he left him until an opportune time" (Luke 4:13). Clearly these temptations Jesus overcame following His baptism were not the only occasions of temptation He faced. For example, later in a private setting with His disciples Jesus explained what was eventually going to happen to Him in Jerusalem. And Peter rebuked Him declaring it would never happen. But Jesus told Peter, "Get behind me, Satan! You are a stumbling block to me; you do not have in mind the concerns of God, but merely human concerns" (Matthew 16:23). Even when Jesus was on the cross a passerby's insult sounded similar to the devil's tests: "Come down from the cross, if you are the Son of God!" (Matthew 27:40).

Following Jesus' death, burial, resurrection, and ascension His followers thought deeply about who He was and all that had taken place. The writer of the New Testament book of Hebrews connects Jesus' temptation experience with His ability to help His followers face their temptations. The Bible is clear that, while we will not all be tested and tempted the way Jesus was, we will all be tempted.

The first key passage that should be a great encouragement to Christians today is Hebrews 2:18 where the author tells believers, "Because he himself suffered when he was tempted, he is able to help those who are being tempted." Jesus has a real connection with us as we face temptation because He experienced it Himself. The difference, of course, is that He never failed the test.

A couple of chapters later, using language from the Old Testament, the writer instructs and challenges believers in Hebrews 4:14: "Therefore, since we have a great high priest who has ascended into heaven, Jesus the Son of God, let us hold firmly to the faith we profess." And then in verses 15 and 16 he makes clear how Jesus can help us: "For we do not have a high priest who is unable to empathize with our weaknesses, but we have one who has been tempted in every way, just as we are—yet he did not sin. Let us then approach God's throne of grace with confidence, so that we may receive mercy and find grace to help us in our time of need." As our high priest, Jesus understands us and provides entrance to the place God sits where we can receive mercy and find grace.

QUESTIONS FOR REFLECTION AND DISCUSSION

1. What do you make of the fact that all three Persons of the Trinity are present at Jesus' baptism?

2. Why was Jesus baptized? What is the connection, if any, with our baptism?

3. What does the Bible mean by the statement "People do not live by bread alone?"

4. Does the fact that Jesus quoted Scripture in the face of temptation tell us anything about how we can face our battles? See Psalm 119:11.

5. Are Christians today ever guilty of "putting God to the test?" What are some examples?

6. How do the passages in Hebrews 2:18 and 4:14-16 encourage you in facing temptation?

CHAPTER TWO

Who Does He Think He Is?

Primary Bible References: Matthew 9:1-8; Mark 2:1-10; and
Luke 5:17-26

W hen unhappy with someone's actions, onlookers often express their displeasure by asking, "Who does he think he is?" The question implies the person has done or said something they are not qualified or authorized to do. That's not exactly the question asked about Jesus in this incident, but that's how it could be paraphrased. And the implication is the same. This questioning of Jesus occurred early in His ministry and was done by "the Pharisees and the teachers of the law" (Luke 5:21). These religious leaders were Jesus' most vocal and persistent critics in the Gospels. We meet them here and will hear from them repeatedly in the chapters that follow.

Context and Setting

This incident took place in a home in Capernaum where so many people had gathered that there was no more room, "not even outside the door" (Mark 2:2). Luke tells us people "had come from every village of Galilee and from Judea and Jerusalem" (5:17). In a short time Jesus had already stirred great interest and a crowd had come not just from the immediate area but from much farther as well—just to see Him and hear Him teach.

Four friends of a paralyzed man brought their friend to Jesus, but because of the crowd could not get him close to Jesus. So they went up on the roof, dug an opening in it, and lowered their friend down on a mat. Mark reports, "When Jesus saw their faith, he said to the paralyzed man, 'Son, your sins are forgiven'" (2:5). Instead of curing the physical problem, Jesus pronounced him forgiven. While that may sound strange to us, it would not have been surprising to those present that day.

Many in the time of Jesus believed there was a direct connection between a person's sin and that person's illness. You may remember that when illness and calamity befell Job his friends came to him and asked him what sin he had committed. And in John 9:2 there is an account of a blind man in which Jesus' disciples asked Him, "Rabbi, who sinned, this man or his parents, that he was born blind?" Some thought a person would not or could not be healed until they had been forgiven of their sin.

We do not know if there was a connection between this man's paralysis and his sin; Jesus did not indicate there was. We don't know why he was paralyzed. We certainly know from Job that all suffering is not the direct result of a person's sin. There were plenty of other times Jesus healed someone without first pronouncing forgiveness of the one He healed. There is more going on in this scene than a connection between sin and illness.

Questioning Jesus

In response to Jesus' pronouncement of forgiveness, the Pharisees and teachers of the law began to question Jesus in their own minds. They were there for a different reason than the rest of the crowd and were among those from Judea and Jerusalem mentioned by Luke. Soon after this incident there was a similar situation in a synagogue. Luke tells us concerning that episode "the Pharisees and teachers of the law were looking for a reason to accuse Jesus, so they watched Him closely" (6:7). I think they were doing the same thing in this situation: keeping an eye on Jesus.

While they didn't say anything out loud, they thought to themselves, "Why does this fellow talk like that? He's blaspheming! Who can forgive sins but God alone?" (Mark 2:7). In other words, "Who does he think he is?" They understood the claim Jesus was making, and He knew what they were thinking.

Let's not confuse the question, "Who can forgive sins but God alone?" Yes, only God can forgive our sins in terms of our guilt before Him. But that truth does not nullify the frequent calls in the New Testament, including from Jesus Himself, for us to forgive those who wrong us. You and I can and should forgive wrongs inflicted upon us by others. And I think we can assure others of God's forgiveness of them, but we cannot forgive on God's behalf.

Considering Jesus' Response

As we would expect, Jesus' response was filled with significance. He did not tell them they were wrong in their premise. He asked them a question to which the answer was obvious: "Which is easier: to say

17

to this paralyzed man, 'Your sins are forgiven,' or to say, 'Get up, take up your mat and walk?'" (Mark 2:9). It is easier to say "Your sins are forgiven" than it is to say "Get up, take your mat and walk." You can't see if someone's sins are forgiven. But it is immediately obvious if a person who could not previously walk gets up and walks.

Not waiting for an answer, Jesus continues, "But I want you to know that the Son of Man has authority on earth to forgive sins" (Mark 2:10). Jesus says in effect, "To prove that I have the authority to forgive sin, I will heal this man." His response to the questioning included more than His words; He would also do something. He told the man, "Get up, take up your mat and go home" (Mark 2:11). And the previously paralyzed man did exactly what Jesus told him to do "in full view of them all" (Mark 2:12a). With that Mark continues, "This amazed everyone and they praised God, saying, 'We have never seen anything like this!'" (verse 12b).

Jesus' authority to forgive was verified and confirmed by the healing. "When the crowd saw this, they were filled with awe; and they praised God, who had given such authority to man" (Matthew 9:8). The fundamental proposition of the religious leaders was right: God alone can forgive sins. They just missed the point: Jesus was not guilty of blasphemy; Jesus could forgive sins because Jesus is God!

Wrap Up

Going back to the beginning of the account, I think we can say friends are important. How thankful the once-paralyzed man must have been for his four friends who took him to Jesus! We don't know much about them, but we have to assume they knew of Jesus and we know they had faith in Him. All of us need friends like that: people who care about us, encourage us, help us, and enrich our lives through their friendship. My life has been enhanced by having friends like that as far back as I can remember. As a matter of fact, it was my best friend in elementary school who first invited me to his church where I became a Christian. It goes without saying that we need to be a friend like that to others.

This is a scene from the Gospels that shows us that faith impresses Jesus. And it wasn't the faith of the man who was healed, it was what his friends did that showed Jesus their faith and impressed Him. Jesus saw their faith (Mark 2:5). I hope our faith is also evident in our actions and results in God being praised.

In the same way Jesus cared about the paralyzed man, Jesus still cares about our bodies and our souls. People sometimes wrongly assume that all Jesus cares about is their spiritual life. That isn't true. He does not always heal, but that does not mean Jesus doesn't care about our bodies. Jesus cares about our bodies, but He cares even more about our souls. He cares so much about our souls that He died on the cross that we might be forgiven.

What He said and did in this account is a claim to divinity. Jesus cured this lame man so that people would know He had the authority to forgive sin. The only reason Jesus' sacrifice on the cross pays the penalty for ours sins, the only way He can provide and offer us forgiveness, is because He is God. I don't completely understand it—how God can be Father, Son, and Holy Spirit—but I believe it because it is what the Bible teaches.

QUESTIONS FOR REFLECTION AND/OR DISCUSSION

1. Can you think of a specific time when someone said or did something others found offensive and you asked the question, "Who do you think you are?" What was the outcome? Were they able to prove they had the authority?

2. Do you find it more exciting when there is a crowd in a class or at church? Is Easter Sunday more exciting for you? Can you imagine the excitement on the day described in this chapter?

3. We can't forgive on behalf of God, but we are called to forgive. What does it mean in the Lord's Prayer when Jesus taught us to pray, "Forgive us our debts, as we also have forgiven our debtors" (Matthew 6:12)?

4. How do we know God cares about our physical bodies as well as our souls? What should it mean to us that God cares about our bodies?

5. Imagine the relationship among these four friends and the paralyzed man. What was it like? What was their motive in taking him to Jesus?

6. Do you have friends like the four friends in the account? Are you that kind of friend to anyone else?

CHAPTER THREE

How Can You Welcome Those Kind of People?

Primary Bible References – Matthew 9:9-13: Mark 2:13-17; and Luke 5:27-32

Most people would agree that who you socialize with is important and says something about you. For instance, parents want their children to hang out with other kids who will have a good influence on them. But although we understand the potential pitfalls of being negatively influenced by others, as Christians we're also taught to connect with others so we can make a positive impact on them by our words and actions.

During His ministry Jesus modeled the practice of interacting with others, primarily by eating with them. And because He regularly spent time with those who were not considered respectable by the Jewish religious establishment, He was criticized and questioned by the religious leaders. There were several groups of religious leaders, but those who criticized Jesus most often were the Pharisees.

Context and Setting

The specific criticism and questioning of Jesus discussed in this chapter began with the calling of Matthew, a tax collector, to be a follower of Jesus. In reading the account it is obvious that as a tax collector, Matthew (called Levi by Luke) would not be considered a good candidate to follow Jesus.

Tax collectors were looked down on and hated for a variety of reasons. They were considered traitors because they worked for the Romans who occupied the land. In addition, they were known to be dishonest and greedy, taking as much money as they could for themselves beyond what tax was required. A window into the system is opened in John the Baptist's reply to tax collectors in response to their question about what they should do; he says, "Don't collect any more than you are required to" (Luke 3:13). Because of these first two factors, tax collectors did not pay much attention to the religious rules many of the Jewish people followed. We'll say more about it later, but the pairing of "tax collectors and sinners" shows how despised they were.

For Jesus to call a man like Matthew to follow Him was totally out of the ordinary and a snub to conventional ideas of respectability. The fishermen He had called earlier (Peter, Andrew, James, and John) were not high on the social scale, but they were not as suspect and low-down as a tax collector.

Perhaps equally significant as the fact that Jesus called Matthew is that Matthew answered the call. We shouldn't think of this as the first time Matthew had encountered Jesus. He undoubtedly knew who Jesus was and had heard Him teach before. When Jesus called he was ready. Luke tells us that Matthew "got up, left everything and followed him" (5:28). Matthew gave up a lot because tax collectors were in the upper class, but it was even more than that. One New Testament scholar notes, "We should not miss the quiet heroism involved in this. If following Jesus had not worked out for the fishermen, they could have returned to their trade without difficulty. But when Matthew walked out of his job he was through."[3]

The setting for the questioning is what happened next. After Matthew responded to Jesus' call he hosted a dinner party for his friends, Jesus, and Jesus' disciples. Luke's Gospel reports, "Levi held a great banquet for Jesus at his house, and a large crowd of tax collectors and others were eating with them" (5:29). Matthew's friends were tax collectors and sinners just like he was! Matthew's Gospel phrases it, "many tax collectors and sinners came and ate with him [Jesus] and his disciples" (9:10).

Questioning Jesus

When Jesus ate with Matthew and his friends, it prompted the Pharisees to question Jesus about hanging out with the wrong kind of people. Matthew 9:11 tells us, "When the Pharisees saw this, they asked his disciples, 'Why does your teacher eat with tax collectors and sinners?'" Luke 5:30 says they "complained to his disciples" asking the same question. Note the Pharisees did not ask Jesus Himself, but His disciples. It makes me think the Pharisees were somewhat cowardly--a lot of critics are. To their credit, however, on other occasions the Pharisees did question Jesus directly. (We'll look as some examples in subsequent chapters.)

However, note that the Pharisees' question to Jesus' disciples really wasn't a question, but a judgement on Him. They didn't want to know why Jesus ate with those kind of people, they wanted His disciples to know they thought it was wrong. Associating with those kind of people was bad enough, but it was altogether something else for Jesus to eat with them. Far more than today, eating with someone in the ancient world suggested tolerance and acceptance. We'll say more about it in chapter five, but for the Pharisees eating with such people would result in ritual defilement.

"Sinners" in the Gospel accounts refers to common people who for a variety of reasons did not or could not follow the elaborate religious rituals the Pharisees followed. The Pharisees scorned those who did not follow their rules and wouldn't have anything to do with them. In the eyes of the religious leaders of Jesus' day they were disreputable people and undesirables; what we might call "the wrong kind of people." The Pharisees were upset that Jesus would associate with people like Matthew and his friends. They viewed it as discrediting Him as a rabbi and making Him out to be a phony. In their view, really righteous people wouldn't do such a thing.

Considering Jesus' Response

Matthew 9:12 notes, "On hearing this, Jesus said" and Luke 5:31 says "Jesus answered them." And what an answer it was! He said, "It is not the healthy who need a doctor, but the sick. I have not come to call the righteous, but sinners." Luke 5:32 adds that Jesus told them He came to call sinners "to repentance." And Matthew 9:13 adds a challenge from Jesus citing Hosea 6:6, "But go and learn what this means: 'I desire mercy, not sacrifice.'" This Old Testament challenge was about going beyond ceremonial obedience.

Please realize that Jesus did not deny the charge--He was eating with tax collectors and sinners. As I heard a preacher say in a Bible study many years ago, "But when you think about it, who else was there to eat with? If He ate with the Pharisees He would still be eating with sinners!" Nor did Jesus apologize; no apology was necessary. In His response Jesus used physical illness as a metaphor for spiritual need. What would be our response to a health care system where doctors would only see people who were healthy? It would be a strange system, wouldn't it? But that is the analogy Jesus used to describe the Pharisees' outlook on Him. They did not understand the purpose of Jesus' coming: apparently they thought the Messiah would condemn the sinful and praise the righteous. But that is not why Jesus came. One of the reasons Jesus was so popular with sinners was that, in the words of Arron Chambers, "the judged found the Judge to be surprisingly nonjudgmental."[4]

In eating with these "sinners" Jesus was not approving of their sin. By His response He indicated the people He was eating with were "sick" --they were indeed "sinners." Remember Luke's account reports Jesus saying, "I have not come to call the righteous, but sinners to repentance" (5:32). Matthew's account doesn't have the same words, but they are implied and understood. From the beginning of both John the Baptist's and Jesus' preaching there was a call to repentance, and the point of calling sinners is not that they should remain the same, but that they may find true righteousness through faith in Jesus. Jesus accepted and welcomed sinners as they were, but He also challenged, encouraged, and empowered them to change. There was another occasion recorded only in Luke 15 in which the religious leaders made the same charge of Jesus welcoming and eating with sinners. And Jesus' response of His three well-known parables of the Lost Sheep, the

Lost Coin, and the Lost Son also demonstrate the purpose of His coming with different images.

Even though Jesus' metaphor confirmed those He ate with were sinners, I do not think He was suggesting the Pharisees were righteous people who were not sick. Do you? I think rather Jesus was emphasizing that they were unaware of their condition. The Pharisees thought they had it all together and were better than everyone else. But they were not as healthy as they thought or as righteous as they appeared. And Jesus certainly was not approving of their blind self-righteousness that resulted in the harsh judgment of others.

Don't forget the part of Jesus' response recorded only in Matthew where He told the Pharisees, "Go and learn what this means: 'I desire mercy, not sacrifice.'" "Go and learn" was a phrase used by teachers to send students back to the Bible to study a passage further. Imagine how taken aback the Pharisees must have been to have Jesus imply they were like first year seminary students. The point of God's Word through the prophet Hosea is that you cannot rely on ritual only and ignore God's internal moral desire. The Pharisees were preoccupied with external ritual purity.

Wrap Up

What does Jesus' response to this questioning mean to us? For one thing, we are not to be like the Pharisees. In general, we are not to focus on the external to the neglect of the internal heart attitude God wants. Specifically, we are not to stay away from or shun the very people Jesus came to heal and save. If just being around sinners was the way sin was transmitted, or it degraded one's relationship with God, Jesus would have been one of the worst sinners of all and not very pleasing to God. The Pharisees could only see the failures of sinners, but Jesus saw their need and wanted to help them. We might ask ourselves if we have isolated ourselves from the people Jesus has called us to reach out to. Are we afraid of those who don't believe as we do, or who hold a political opinion different from ours, or who don't carry out their faith as we do? If we are, we have missed the point of Jesus' coming.

We are not to be like the Pharisees; we are to be like Jesus. He did not look down on and separate Himself from those who weren't religious. Just as Jesus came to call sinners, He sends Christians today to witness for Him. He gives us the same commission He gave His closest followers after His resurrection: "As the Father has sent me, I am sending you" (John 20:21). In terms of His teaching in the Sermon on the Mount Jesus calls us to be both salt and light (Mathew 5:13-16). And we can only do what He has asked us to do by being in contact with those we are commissioned to influence. We have to be in the world so we can connect and build bridges of friendship with those who need a "doctor." We cannot look down on those who need the Lord and come across as though we have it all together and are better than they are. The reason people like Matthew and his friends were attracted to Jesus is because of the way He saw them and treated them. He saw their potential.

You and I are sinners called by Jesus to follow Him. He can only help us if we acknowledge our need and admit we are sick and need a doctor. And admitting our need is not something that happens only at the beginning of the Christian life. Nor is repenting of our sin something that happens only at the beginning of our walk with Jesus. Since we will never reach perfection, we will always need Jesus and need to regularly repent of our sins.

Of all the designations given to Jesus, none is more attractive than the label His enemies gave Him—that He was "a friend of tax collectors and sinners" (Matthew 11:19 and Luke 7:14). Aren't you glad Jesus is a friend of sinners? Aren't you glad He is your friend? Jesus is still calling people to follow Him today—unlikely candidates like Matthew and sinners like you and me. And people are still responding to follow Him. We call them Christians.

QUESTIONS FOR REFLECTION AND/OR DISCUSSION

1. In your experience, have you had a greater influence on your unbelieving friends or have they had a greater influence on you? Can you give some examples?

2. Why do you think Matthew gave up his lucrative job to follow Jesus?

3. Why do you suppose Jesus' critics went to His disciples instead of Him?

4. Why did Jesus use a metaphor about physical health when describing his ministry?

5. Have you ever been accused of approving of someone's less than ideal lifestyle because you hung out with them?

6. What was Jesus praying for in John 17:15: "My prayer is not that you take them out of the world but that you protect them from the evil one?"

CHAPTER FOUR

Don't You Care?

Primary Bible References - Matthew 8:23-27; Mark 4:35-31; and Luke 8:22-25

With the exception of this chapter, all the other incidents discussed in this book are occasions when Jesus' critics questioned Him trying to test, discredit, trap, trick, and delegitimize Him. The incident to be explored in this chapter, however, does not involve His critics. It is rather His followers who question Him.

In Mark's account of this incident the disciples asked Jesus, "Don't you care?" (4:38). The actual question is longer than that, but that's the gist of it. Unlike all the other questioning of Jesus we are examining, this question was not about testing or tricking Him. But although the disciples were not questioning Jesus as a way to trap him, they were certainly doing more than seeking information.

"Don't you care?" is a question a lot of people still ask the Lord today, both unbelievers and believers alike. Even if you have never asked it, I suspect there have been times in your life when you have thought it. That's why I think this chapter will be especially helpful to all of us.

Context and Setting

Mark tells us this episode took place in the evening following a day of Jesus teaching. At Jesus' suggestion they all crossed the lake (according to Luke 8:22) or the sea (according to Matthew 8:23). In the midst of the trip a severe storm developed, raising concern with the disciples. Because of the low altitude and the surrounding hills, sudden storms still hit the Sea of Galilee today.

I note that the storm raised concern with the disciples without mentioning Jesus because He was asleep. Jesus was asleep because He was tired. I don't think for a minute Jesus was pretending to be asleep in order to teach the disciples a lesson. This is another indication that although Jesus was and is the Son of God, He was also fully human. There are a variety of places in the New Testament where it is clear Jesus faced the same kind of physical realities we all face in terms of hunger, thirst, and the need for rest. If you ever wonder if Jesus can identify with your fatigue, the answer is yes!

In the face of the situation the disciples determined to wake Jesus—that tells us how strong this storm actually was. At least four of the disciples were experienced fishermen and used to these kinds of storms; they would certainly know when they were in trouble. According to Mark the squall was furious and the waves were breaking over the boat, threatening to sink it. On top on the severity of the storm, this was taking place at night. We never read in the Bible of the disciples interrupting Jesus' prayer time, but here they do wake Him from His sleep. Apparently they had enough faith in Jesus to believe that if He was awake He could save them, but not enough to ride the storm out while He was asleep.

Questioning Jesus

Mark 4:38 tells us they woke Jesus and asked, "Teacher, don't you care if we drown?" There is a tone of irritation and reproach in what they asked. It reminds me of Martha's question to Jesus in Luke 10:40: "Don't you care that my sister has left me to do the work by myself?" She follows this question by telling Jesus what do to; she says to Him, "Tell her to help me." The disciples did not tell Jesus what to do, but it was implied He needed to do something. Even though they were afraid, and as inadequate as their faith may have been, the fact that they woke Jesus indicates they did have faith in Him.

Considering Jesus' Response

Jesus' response to the disciples' questioning was twofold. Matthew, Mark, and Luke all report He calmed the storm and questioned the disciples. Matthew, however, has Jesus asking the question first (8:26), while Mark (4:40) and Luke (8:25) have Jesus questioning them after He calmed the storm. Mark also reports Jesus asking them two questions.

Even though this book is not about apologetics and defending the reliability of the Gospels, I want to comment on the discrepancies among the three accounts. (And remember it is only Mark who reports the disciples asking, "Teacher, don't you care if we drown?") For me these minor differences underscore the reliability of the record. If the writers of the Gospels were in collusion and making things up, they certainly would have gotten their stories straight before writing them down. In addition, if the authors of the Gospels were conspiring to give the best possible account, it seems unusual that only Matthew and Luke omitted the disciples' questioning of Jesus. Wouldn't Mark have wanted to eliminate this detail as well so as not to make the disciples look bad? Instead, the Gospels are full of these small discrepancies as well as incident after incident in which the disciples look foolish or unbelieving. In my mind, this is evidence that they should be trusted as authentic accounts written without an agenda other than telling people the good news of Christ.[5]

In response to being awakened Jesus did calm the storm. Mark reports, "He got up, rebuked the wind and said to the waves, 'Quiet! Be still!' Then the wind died down and it was completely calm" (4:39). All three accounts report a similar response from the disciples: "The men were amazed and asked, 'What kind of man is this? Even the winds and the waves obey him!'" (Matthew 8:27). They were amazed, as in the presence of God. They saw and knew that He was a man, but now they also knew He was more than just a man. Managing nature in terms of the storm and sea was something only God could do. They were coming more and more to understand that He was the Son of God. This entire incident is often pointed to as underscoring in quick succession both the humanity as well as the divinity of Jesus. We see human weariness in His sleeping and the divine voice ruling nature.

Whether Jesus calmed the storm before He spoke to His disciples or not, He did scold them and ask a convicting question: "You of little faith, why are you so afraid?" The answer to His question is suggested in His address "you of little faith." Jesus wasn't miffed that His disciples woke Him, He was disappointed they didn't have more faith. After all, by this time they had seen Him do quite a bit and had heard Him teach often; He expected their faith would have been stronger.

Wrap Up

This exchange between Jesus and His disciples challenges us to think about our faith. It would be difficult to overstate the importance of faith in the Christian life. Hebrews 11:6 declares, "And without faith it is impossible to please God, because anyone who comes to him must believe that he exists and that he rewards those who earnestly seek him." We are saved by faith; or in other words, we become Christians by faith. Not only are we saved by faith, however, we are also to live by faith. Jesus repeatedly made this point in His teaching as does both the Old Testament and the New Testament. And living by faith means that faith is something in which we grow. In His words to His disciples Jesus was challenging them to greater faith and He does the same to us today.

One thing we might suggest from this entire episode is that storms are a part of life. In a printed message by Rick Warren he notes storms "are inevitable, they are unpredictable, and they are impartial. They're going to come, we're not sure when, and we're all going to face them."

Isn't it interesting that in this account the disciples were in a storm because they were following Jesus? It was His idea to go across the lake. Perhaps the disciples expected everything to be smooth sailing because they were with Him. Being a Christian and following Jesus does not guarantee cloudless skies or smooth sailing in life. Sometimes being a follower of Jesus leads us into storms. I don't think the storm this particular evening surprised Jesus, do you? The reality is nothing ever surprises God.

Just like the disciples we sometimes wonder if Jesus really cares. We sometimes believe Jesus has let us down. God does not always perform miracles to rescue us from life's storms. And there are false teachers who wrongly suggest that if we had more faith we would be saved from the storms of life; we would be healed, our marriage would not fail, our financial woes would be resolved, or our child would not suffer. But that is cruel and not what the Bible teaches. Real faith trusts God in the storm no matter what the outcome. There is also a connection between fear and faith. As we grow in faith, fear becomes less a factor in our lives.

Considering Jesus' assessment of the disciples, "You of little faith" (Matthew 8:26), we must ask ourselves how much faith is enough. I'm not sure I know. Probably just like you, I'm still trying to cultivate my faith and root out fear in my life. One thing we might note, there is no record of Jesus ever telling anyone they had too much faith! How much faith is enough? I don't know, but I suspect you and I both could use a little more. The point is that Jesus can be trusted, especially in the storms of life.

I read that one day Mark Twain and a friend walked outside in the rain. The friend asked him, "Do you think it will stop?" And Twain responded, "It always does." That's true with any storm. You've got to go through it, but it's not going to last forever. Eventually, or ultimately, it will end.

QUESTIONS FOR REFLECTION AND/OR DISCUSSION

1. Are you at all surprised by the disciples' fear in this account? Why or why not?

2. Do you think Jesus was really asleep, or was He "faking it?"

3. When the disciples woke Jesus and asked Him their question, do you think they thought He would or could calm the storm?

4. Have there been times in your life when you asked the Lord the question, "Don't you care?" Can you give a specific example? Was it related to fear in any way?

5. How have you been able to strengthen and grow in your faith?

6. What's going on in Psalm 23:4 when David says, "Even though I walk through the darkest valley (the valley of the shadow of death) I will fear no evil, for you are with me; your rod and staff, they comfort me?" What does this verse mean to you?

CHAPTER FIVE

Why Don't You Follow Our Traditions?

Primary Bible References – Matthew 15:1-20 and Mark 7:1-23

One of the most common questions parents ask their children before they eat is, "Did you wash your hands?" It may be surprising to some to learn that the Pharisees and teachers of the law were critical of Jesus' disciples because they didn't wash their hands before eating. But for those religious leaders it wasn't about germs and cleanliness. It was about ceremony and tradition.

Tradition in and of itself is not a bad thing. The way a tradition is used and understood determines whether it is beneficial or harmful. It's the misuse of tradition that makes it bad. The Pharisees and teachers of the law provide an example of misunderstanding and misuse of tradition. The incident to be examined in this study is but one example of several from the Gospels, but can serve to shed light on the others as well.

Context and Setting

The situation for this exchange between the religious leaders and Jesus is similar to other scenes in the gospel accounts. Jesus' popularity had continued to grow, with many people wanting to be near Him.

Mark tells us, "The Pharisees and some of the teachers of the law who had come from Jerusalem gathered around Jesus" (7:1). We aren't told why they came, but the fact that they came so far suggests we can be fairly sure it was to keep an eye on Him. And if that is true, they saw something to criticize. They saw some of Jesus' disciples eating with unwashed hands.

Mark gives readers the background for what followed. "The Pharisees and all the Jews do not eat unless they give their hands a ceremonial washing, holding to the tradition of the elders. When they come from the marketplace they do not eat unless they wash" (7:3 and 4a). Note the phrases ceremonial washing and the tradition of the elders. The practice went even further than described here, but it is this tradition that set the stage for the questioning.

Questioning Jesus

The question the Pharisees and teachers of the law asked Jesus was not about His actions, but rather His disciples' actions. Matthew 15:2 reports the question: "Why do your disciples break the tradition of the elders? They don't wash their hands before they eat!" They asked Jesus because as their rabbi He was somewhat responsible for their actions. Their complaint was that by not washing their hands before eating, the disciples were breaking the tradition of the elders, and when they did so they were "eating their food with defiled hands" (Mark 7:5).

The Pharisees' concern was ritual cleanliness. The practice came from the Old Testament law in which priests were required to be washed (ritually clean) before they carried out their duties in leading worship. With the passing of time leaders among the Jews expanded and added to many of the Old Testament laws. There was the written Law that was Scripture and there was the oral Law that had developed. The motivation in developing these traditions was good; it was to honor God by protecting His law. It was thought of in terms of "building a fence" around the law to make sure it was not broken. But the tradition had become so expanded and convoluted it became a burden. The key to the question was in the phrase "break the tradition of the elders" (Matthew 15:2). The tradition of the elders came from man and was not the Law of God.

Considering Jesus' Response

Both Matthew and Mark give Jesus' extended response, but begin differently. Mark begins by citing the Old Testament prophet Isaiah before challenging the Pharisees. Matthew, however, gives the challenge first and quotes Isaiah afterwards. In His response Jesus addressed three different audiences: His questioners, the crowd, and finally His disciples.

As Matthew reports (15:3), Jesus did not directly answer their question. He responded by asking a question that must have put them on the defensive: "And why do you break the command of God for the sake of your tradition?" (Matthew 15:3). Before they could answer Jesus gave the example of how they manipulated another tradition to violate the fifth commandment, the one to honor your father and mother. Matthew quotes Jesus: "You say that if anyone declares what might have been used to help their father and mother is 'devoted to God,' they are not to 'honor their father or mother' with it" (15:5 and 6a). This tradition declared that anything dedicated to God became out of reach to be used for others. In Jesus' example the tradition was used to bypass the commandment to honor one's parents by helping

41

them financially. Jesus' conclusion was, "Thus you nullify the word of God for the sake of your tradition" (15:6b). The oral Law was being used to circumvent the written Law. He continued by calling them hypocrites and quoting Isaiah 29:13 about people honoring God with their lips and not their hearts by following mere human rules and not God's law.

After speaking to His critics Jesus called the crowd and made a public pronouncement in which He gave the foundational principle, "What goes into someone's mouth does not defile them, but what comes out of the mouth, that is what defiles them" (Matthew 15:11). He stressed the truth that defilement is not about ritual and external behavior but rather what is moral and internal.

The third wave of Jesus' response was a private explanation to His disciples. They asked Him what must have been obvious to everyone, "Do you know that the Pharisees were offended when they heard this?" (Matthew 15:12). Jesus' response was one of His better-known sayings, "They are blind guides. If the blind lead the blind, both will fall into a pit" (Matthew 15:14).

Then Peter asked Jesus to explain the parable, referring to the foundational principle Jesus gave in verse 11. Jesus began His response with an elementary lesson about the digestive system: "Don't you see that whatever enters the mouth goes into the stomach and then out of the body?" (Matthew 15:17). I think it is worth the space to quote the rest of Jesus' response in verses 18-20: "But the things that come out of a person's mouth come from the heart, and these defile them. For out of the heart come evil thoughts—murder, adultery, sexual immorality, theft, false testimony, slander. These are what defile a person; but eating with unwashed hands does not defile them."

Wrap Up

Jesus made it clear tradition does not have the same level of authority as biblical teaching. Note again the contrast Jesus drew in Matthew 15:3 between "the command of God" and "your tradition." Note also the contrast in verses 4 and 5 between "God said" and "you say." Since tradition does not have the authority of Scripture, it cannot override God's commands or be used to violate them.

As we noted in the introduction of this chapter, tradition is not a bad thing. It's the misuse of tradition that makes it bad. I'm not aware of situations in Bible-believing churches today where traditions are used to go against the clear desire of the Lord for His people. But I am aware of some traditions that people cling to as though the tradition itself is the clear will of God. We must be careful and guard against equating our traditions with what the Bible clearly commands of God's people.

As important as the discussion about tradition and biblical authority was, Jesus used the questioning to go beyond that basic issue to speak about defilement and purity. Those who questioned Jesus were concerned about outward ceremonial defilement and purity. But Jesus focused on what really matters, the heart.

Referring not to the physical organ, but to the seat of a person's thought and will, Jesus pointed out that physical food does not affect the heart. His point was that it is not about what we eat but who we are. Defilement doesn't come from the outside, it comes from the inside. And while our physical hearts can be diseased and damaged, Jesus was talking about serious spiritual heart conditions. The error of the

Pharisees was they focused on a person's unwashed hands instead of looking to the heart.

Real purity is not about going through all the right motions, it's about getting our hearts right. That isn't to suggest we shouldn't do the right things. It is to affirm that having our hearts right includes more than just going through the motions; it also includes the right motive.

Jesus wants us to know that it is both the attitudes and behaviors coming from the heart that defile a person. What do you think about this list of things Jesus says defile us? Do you ever struggle with any of these? I don't know about you, but I don't measure up when I allow Jesus to tell me what makes a person unclean. It would be far easier to simply wash our hands before we eat, wouldn't it?

QUESTIONS FOR REFLECTION AND/OR DISCUSSION

1. Does your family have some traditions they follow for holidays or special occasions?

2. In terms of the Church and the Christian life, what are some good things about tradition and what are some dangers to avoid? Can you give examples of both?

3. Are there some things Christians today get mixed up on in terms of external and internal defilement?

4. How does Jesus' teaching in the Sermon on the Mount about murder and adultery relate to His teaching in this passage? (Matthew 5:21-30)

5. What can we do when we realize our hearts are not pure?

6. How can we guard our hearts in terms of keeping them pure?

CHAPTER SIX

"What Do You Say?"

Bible Reference – John 7:53-8:11

Some sins seem worse and make us more uncomfortable than others, and for many Christians adultery is at the top of the list. In high school many of us had to read Nathaniel Hawthorne's classic novel The Scarlet Letter. It's the chilling story about a young married woman named Hester who is punished for committing adultery by being forced to wear a scarlet "A" on the front of her clothing. I'm sure even those who have not committed adultery are glad that punishment is not carried out today.

In this chapter we see Jesus being questioned about an act of adultery. However, even though adultery is the premise for this question, it's not really the main point. The main point of the exchange is testing and trying to trap Jesus, and we see a great contrast between Jesus and those who questioned Him.

Before turning to the passage we should note it does have textual issues. Most Bibles include some indication in the margin or in a footnote that these verses do not appear in the earliest and best manuscripts. As you probably know, prior to the invention of the printing press all copies of the Bible were handwritten. In publishing the Bible today scholars compare all of the available copies and try to put together the best text they can. Scholars agree that the story we're focusing on today was not in the oldest copies of John and was inserted later.

But to say that this account is not an original part of John's Gospel does not mean it did not happen. I'm convinced this is a true scene from Jesus' ministry. It is consistent with what we know from the rest of the Gospels about Jesus and the religious leaders. As one New Testament scholar observes, "The story has an authentic ring to it. As we read it we feel, 'This is what Jesus would have said.'"[6]

Context and Setting

The account opens with Jesus sitting in the temple courts teaching. Unlike today, in the culture of the time teachers usually sat when they taught. Like many other occasions people gathered around Jesus to hear Him. But this teaching session, like some others, was interrupted.

The teachers of the law and the Pharisees brought a women caught in adultery, made her stand before everyone, and questioned Jesus. John gives us their motive in verse 6: "They were using this question as a trap, in order to have a basis for accusing him." The religious leaders always seemed to be on the lookout for a way to discredit Jesus. Why? I think because people were always gathering around Him and His popularity made them jealous. They saw themselves as the teachers of religion and were threatened by Jesus and His teaching

Questioning Jesus

The question they asked Jesus was a good one given their purpose: "Teacher, this woman was caught in the act of adultery. In the law Moses commanded us to stone such women. Now what do you say?" (verses 4 and 5). Note how polite they were in their address, calling Jesus "teacher" as they would any rabbi. But that was part of the set-up. During this time if a difficult legal question arose the natural and routine thing was to take it to a rabbi for a decision. And so they brought this woman to him, caught in the act of adultery, and asked Jesus if He agreed with the Law of Moses that she should be stoned. They thought they had set the perfect trap to embarrass Jesus, because they assumed He had two options and either one he chose would discredit him.

One option was Jesus could agree with them and say, "Stone her." If He did that He would have two problems: one with the people and one with the government. As the occupiers of the territory, the Romans did not give the Jews the right to put anyone to death. (As you may recall, that was part of the problem later on for the religious leaders when they were trying to have Jesus put to death.) If Jesus approved the execution of this woman He would have been in trouble with the Roman authorities. But beyond that, He would have lost His connection with the people as one who cared about sinners. Adultery wasn't all that rare and people weren't being executed for it. Had Jesus approved of stoning this woman, even if it hadn't been carried out, He would no longer have been viewed as "a friend of sinners."

Jesus' other option was to say, "No, don't stone her." But if He said that they would have accused Him of not believing and following

49

God's law. They would have charged Him with relaxing God's requirements. The religious elite had already concluded from previous observations that Jesus was "soft on sinners."

What was Jesus to do? Those who tried to trap Him underestimated Jesus and never imagined a third option.

Considering Jesus' Response

It is striking that when they first questioned Jesus He remained silent. Verse 6b tells us, "Jesus bent down and started to write on the ground." They wanted to trap Him and He simply stooped and wrote on the ground. What He wrote we can only conjecture; I have read a variety of suggestions, but no one knows. Likewise we can only guess why He did this. He may have wanted time to think; He may have wanted them to repeat their charges so that they might realize what they were doing; or it may have been because He did not want to look at these religious leaders who were acting so cruelly and therefore hid the anger that flushed His face. But Jesus didn't say a thing.

I think Jesus' silence only served to heighten the anticipation of those who thought they would discredit Him. "When they kept on questioning him," verse 7 continues, "He straightened up and said to them, 'Let any one of you who is without sin be the first to throw a stone at her.'" And then be stooped again and wrote on the ground. They wanted Jesus to answer their question, but instead His words pierced their hearts. Jesus said in effect, "All right, stone her. But let the one who is perfect be the first to throw a stone."

What Jesus said could not possibly be construed as a rejection of the Law; He agreed with the Law. But His limitation on who might

50

throw the first stone prevented any harm from coming to her. I'm taken aback that after Jesus made His statement He again stooped and wrote in the dirt. He did not chide His critics or "twist the knife" so to speak; He was not interested in humiliating them. And so in keeping with Middle East culture of looking to their elders, they walked away one at a time from the oldest to the youngest. Whatever else the Pharisees might have said or taught, they knew they were not perfect.

But the woman was still there and Jesus' words to her give us more insight into His attitude than perhaps anything else in the drama. He stood again and asked her, "Woman, where are they? Has no one condemned you?" (verse 10). And she politely answered that no one was there to do so. Jesus responded, "Then neither do I condemn you. Go now and leave your life of sin" (verse 11). The one person in the world who had the right to condemn her didn't. Jesus was willing to give her another chance.

However, even though Jesus did not condemn her, he did challenge her. He called her to give up her life of sin. And in doing that He expressed hope in her future; He knew she could do better. There are those who feel this woman got off too easily; that Jesus treated her sin lightly. And it certainly is possible that Jesus could be misunderstood. That very well may be why this episode was omitted from the oldest manuscripts—some may have felt this story would be misunderstood as Jesus downplaying her sin so they left it out. But Jesus did not say the woman's sin should be glossed over; nor did He say it could be lightly forgiven. Remember Jesus was going to the cross to pay the penalty for sin--hers and yours and mine.

Wrap Up

Let's conclude with some observations about those who questioned Jesus. One thing that stands out in this story was their cruelty to this woman. They showed her no sensitivity, making her stand in front of everyone as they carried out their scheme. And consider their inconsistency. She "was caught in the act of adultery," but her partner, who was equally guilty and should have been brought along as well, was absent. They used God's Word for their own end—as a means of discrediting Jesus. There was no real concern for righteousness; they simply wanted to trap Jesus. Finally, it seems obvious that until Jesus called them on it, they were blind to their own sins. They saw the shortcomings of others, but not their own—sins of attitude and the heart.

Everything the Pharisees were, Jesus was not. And everything Jesus was, they were not. We must guard ourselves against being cruel to others, especially in public, and against humiliating them. We must strive to be consistent in our evaluation of others, not picking on some and ignoring others. We must guard against misusing the Bible--quoting it only to serve our own purposes and ignoring the parts that speak to our own lives. And we must not close our eyes to our own shortcomings. In short, we must learn to be more like Jesus.

QUESTIONS FOR REFLECTION AND/OR DISCUSSION

1. Do Christians today tend to see some sins as worse than others? Which ones? Are some sins worse than others?

2. Do you think my observation about why this episode is not in the earliest manuscripts makes sense?

3. How telling is it about the culture that this woman was brought to Jesus but her partner was not?

4. Why do you think Jesus stooped and wrote in the sand?

5. Why do you think Jesus did not ridicule His critics as they dropped their stones and left?

6. Do you think this woman got off too easy?

CHAPTER SEVEN

"Show Us a Sign"

Primary Bible References – Matthew 12:38-40, 16:1-4; Mark 8:11-13;
Luke 11:16, 29-32;12:54-56; and John 2:18-22

There are many different kinds of signs. Advertisers use signs to draw attention to all kinds of products. The freeways in Southern California are filled with signs to help drivers. In baseball the catcher gives the pitcher signs and the third base coach gives the batters and base runners signs. Some people use sign language for communicating with the deaf and hard of hearing.

Signs are important. But the meaning of a sign is not always clear and signs can be misinterpreted. All of us have probably given signs to others that have been misunderstood as well as been confused by the signs of others.

One of the ways Jesus' critics questioned Him was by asking for a sign from heaven. They pressed Him on this matter on multiple occasions. New Testament scholar Leon Morris reports, "Their demand arose from the fact that the Jews were a very practical race and that they expected God to perform mighty miracles when the messianic age dawned."[7]

Context and Setting

Since Jesus was asked for a sign on multiple occasions, there are several contexts in which the questioning was carried out. Matthew records two situations, one of which was probably the same as the one included in Mark, and the other the same as the one recorded by Luke. The incident John tells us about was probably unique to his Gospel. This variety makes sense in that Jesus was presented with the same challenge more than once. He repeated Himself on different occasions with minor variations, and the Gospel writers were free to select and arrange their material as they saw fit.

John's account of the request for a sign was presented to Jesus after He had driven the animals out of the temple and overturned the tables of the money changers (John 2:13-18). The accounts in Matthew 12 and Luke 11 follow a scene in which Jesus had driven out a demon. The accounts in Matthew 16 and Mark 8 come soon after Jesus fed 4000 people with seven loaves and a few small fish.

Questioning Jesus

The request in John 2 was in response to the well-known incident when Jesus cleared the temple: "What sign can you show us to prove your authority to do all this?" (verse 18). The reason "others tested him by asking for a sign from heaven" (Luke 11:16) was because the Pharisees and others suggested, "It is only by Beelzebub, the prince of demons, that this fellow drives out demons" (Matthew 12:24). After the feeding of the 4000, both Matthew 16:1 and Mark 8:11 report the Pharisees (and Sadducees in Matthew) tested Him by asking for a sign from heaven—something that proved He came from God.

The gist of all these requests for a sign suggests Jesus' questioners were looking for some verification that He was, in fact, qualified and authorized to do what He was doing. You cannot help but wonder what the skeptics thought Jesus' expulsion of the demon or His feeding of the 5000 represented. In chapter 10 we will come to a similar line of questioning during Jesus' final week when His critics omit asking for a sign and simply ask about the source of His authority. In these earlier requests for a sign His questioners are probably also hoping to discredit and disqualify Jesus in the eyes of the crowd. That is why in the questioning after the feeding of the 4000 they stressed they wanted a sign from heaven.

Mark indicates that Jesus "sighed deeply" in response to the request for a sign (8:12). One commentator notes this showed Jesus' disappointment "towards lack of faith in those who might be expected to possess it.... Thus it is clear that unbelief lay at the root of the Pharisaic attitude."[8]

Jesus' Response

In every instance Jesus refused the request. But beyond that common response there was some variety. In Matthew 16 and Luke 12 Jesus pointed out how they could see signs to forecast the weather, but they could not "interpret the signs of the times" (Matthew 16:4). The religious leaders would have been expected to believe. They should have seen God's hand in Jesus' actions but they were oblivious to the big picture of what was happening through His coming and ministry. They didn't see it because they didn't want to see it. Others, including Jesus' disciples, did see it and came to faith in Jesus.

Because they were seeking a sign, Jesus called them "a wicked and adulterous generation" in both Matthew 12:39 and 16:4. In Mark 8:12 Jesus simply said, "No sign will be given." It reminds me of Satan's temptations following Jesus' baptism when he challenged Jesus to prove He was the Son of God. Jesus had already rejected the challenge to win followers by impressing them with God's power.

In Matthew 12:4, Matthew 16:4, and Luke 11:29 Jesus told them no sign would be given except the sign of Jonah. In Matthew 12:40 Jesus further explained: "For as Jonah was three days and nights in the belly of a huge fish, so the Son of Man will be three days in the heart of this earth." He was referring, of course, to His future death, burial, and resurrection. After His resurrection, of course, it became central in declaring Jesus as the Christ.

In the exchange in John's Gospel Jesus said, "Destroy this temple, and I will raise it again in three days" (2:19) The Jews did not understand what Jesus meant, thinking He was referring to the temple, but John notes "the temple he had spoken of was his body" (2:21). John concludes the episode: "After he was raised from the dead, his disciples recalled what he had said. Then they believed the scripture and the words that Jesus had spoken" (2:22).

Reading about Jesus' resurrection in terms of the sign of Jonah and the raising of the temple reminds me of Jesus' parable of the Rich Man and Lazarus in Luke 16:19-31. In the story, following their deaths, poor Lazarus goes to Abraham's side and the rich man to a place of torment. The rich man asks Abraham to send Lazarus to warn his brothers about the place of torment. When Abraham tells him they have Moses and the Prophets the rich man suggests if someone from the dead would go to them they would repent. But Abraham responded, "If they do not listen to Moses and the prophets, they will not be convinced even if someone rises from the dead."

Wrap Up

Citing all of these references may have complicated this chapter, but they all relate to the same line of questioning. And while Jesus' response was not always exactly the same, He did give the same basic answer.

As we saw in the first chapter of this book discussing Satan's temptations, Jesus was not going to be the kind of Messiah who would use His divine powers for His own purposes. Jesus did not perform miracles to impress anyone or prove anything. But He did perform signs. After He changed water into wine John tells us, "What Jesus did here in Cana of Galilee was the first of the signs through which he revealed his glory; and his disciples believed in him" (2:11). Later, speaking of those who refused to believe, John tells us, "Even after Jesus had performed so many signs in their presence, they still would not believe in him" (12:37). And even though He did not do miracles in order prove Himself, both Jesus and John expected those who witnessed the signs would come to faith in Him (see John 20:30 and 31).

Jesus is still looking for people to put their faith in Him today. He is not inclined to perform a sign to elicit faith, although those with a perceptive eye can see signs of His involvement in the world and in their lives. But God is not going to prove Himself to anyone.

As a pastor, one thing that concerns me is believers looking for a sign to confirm God's specific will for their lives. Going back to the

Old Testament hero Gideon in Judges 6:36-40, the Bible speaks of Gideon "putting out the fleece" in search of a sign from God. And God answered Gideon's request. But Gideon's was a special case. [9] The Bible does not teach that we are to seek signs to know what God's will is. God has given us a variety of helps to determine His will, but asking for a sign is not one of them.

Finally, recalling Jesus' response to requests for a sign, the sign of significance today is still His resurrection from the grave. Jesus' resurrection authenticated His person, His life, and the teaching and work He had come to accomplish.

QUESTIONS FOR REFLECTION AND/OR DISCUSSION

1. Why do you think Jesus' critics asked for a sign from Him?

2. Have you ever asked God for a sign to prove His existence? Or do you know of others who have? Do such questions represent a lack of faith?

3. Was it reasonable for Jesus to use His resurrection as a sign even before it happened?

4. Have you ever asked God for a sign to confirm direction in your life with regard to His will?

5. What is the difference between asking for a sign and being alert to circumstances in one's life?

6. Is Jesus' resurrection still an adequate sign today for putting one's faith in Him?

CHAPTER EIGHT

"Who Is My Neighbor?"

Primary Bible Reference – Luke 10:25-37

T rue or fiction, joke or novel, movie or TV show, everyone enjoys a good story. In this chapter we come to an exchange in which Jesus tells a great story.

Jesus told a lot of stories in His teaching ministry. They are often called parables, and the story we're considering in this chapter is one of Jesus' best-known and most-loved parables. It is an episode that is found only in Luke's Gospel.

Context and Setting

The setting for the questioning in this chapter is somewhat similar to the questioning we will consider in chapter twelve. The question is asked by "an expert in the law" (Luke 10:25). "Expert in the law" refers to a scholar who was a specialist in what we know today as the Old Testament. The fact that he wanted "to test Jesus" tells us he wanted to argue religion. We have all probably talked with people who wanted to argue about the Bible and religion. Sometimes those who want to argue about the Bible are trying to flaunt their knowledge. Others, however, like to argue so they can keep Christianity at arm's length. This lawyer wanted to "test Jesus."

His first question was, "Teacher, what must I do to inherit eternal life?" And it was a challenging question. Imagine how surprised he must have been when Jesus answered his question with a question: "What is written in the Law? How do you read it?" (verse 26). Similar to what we saw in chapter three, this "expert in the law" must have been taken aback to be interrogated like a student and have Jesus imply he was asking something he should already know.

He gave a correct and commendable answer: "'Love the Lord your God with all your heart, with all your soul, with all your strength, and with all your mind'; and, 'Love your neighbor as yourself'" (verse 27). It's the same combination of Old Testament teaching that Jesus gave in Matthew 22 in answer to the question, "Which is the greatest commandment?" (See chapter twelve.) He showed his expertise by putting these two commandments together. He knew his Bible. Jesus commended him, "You have answered correctly. Do this and you will live" (verse 28).

Questioning Jesus

We've already noted the first question that gives us the context and setting and Jesus' answer. But this expert in the law was not satisfied with his answer and Jesus' approval of it. His first question had presented no problem to Jesus, and that led to the question that is the focus of this chapter.

Luke tells us he wanted to justify himself so he asked Jesus, "And who is my neighbor?" (verse 29). I don't think he was pursuing his test of Jesus with this question; instead, it was now personal in terms of his own life. He knew he wasn't living up to the commandments he had cited. He knew he didn't love God with everything he was. And he knew he didn't love his neighbors as he should. So in order to justify himself, he seems to want to limit the field of those who were his neighbors. After all, that meant he was "off the hook" in terms of who he was required to love. As an expert in the law he probably thought Jesus would give a list of those he was to love and he might find a loophole. How wrong he was.

Considering Jesus' Response

In reply to the question "Who is my neighbor?" Jesus told His great story of the Good Samaritan. You can read it in your Bible and we will summarize it here. It's about a man who was robbed, stripped, beaten up, and left along the side of the road. A priest came by, saw the man, and went by on the other side. Next a Levite came by, saw the man and also passed by. Apparently they did not see the victim as a neighbor they were called to love.

Then the hero of the story—a Samaritan—came by. He saw the man, had compassion on him, and took pity on him. That is, he treated his wounds, put the man on his own donkey, and took him to an inn. The next morning he paid the innkeeper, asked him to care for the man, and promised he would return and pay any additional costs.

The first two people who came by the victim, the priest and the Levite, were religious figures. Both of these men were committed to obeying every aspect of the law, and they were people you would expect to help. That is still true today. Not long ago I was guest preaching at a church in Los Angeles and that morning there were three homeless people who came looking for help. The many years I was a pastor we often had people in need stop by the church building or call and request help. Most people expect those who are religious to be willing to help those in need.

There were probably many reasons these two religious leaders could have given for not helping. Many observers suggest it had to do with their desire not to become ceremonially unclean. (Remember we introduced this concept in chapter five.) But whatever reason they might have given, they couldn't say they didn't see the man. In His story Jesus made it clear they both saw the victim. But having seen him, they passed by on the other side.

Those who heard Jesus tell this story would have expected the next passerby to be a "regular" Jewish layperson. That would be logical in terms of the order. But the third person to come along, the hero of the story, was an outsider—a Samaritan. There was a bitterness and even hatred between Jews and Samaritans that went all the way back to the seventh century B.C. This Samaritan was the last person those who heard the story would have expected to help a Jew. But he did. He took pity on the man who had been beaten, robbed, and left.

Jesus did not directly answer the question, "Who is my neighbor?" Instead, he told the story. And having told the story, He asked His questioner, "Which of these do you think was a neighbor to the man who fell into the hands of the robbers?" (verse 36). There was only one possible answer and the expert gave it: "The one who had mercy on him" (verse 37a). To which Jesus responded, "Go and do likewise" (verse 37b). There was no scolding from Jesus, just a clear challenge. His story suggests that the answer to the question "Who is my neighbor?" is anyone who is in need.

Wrap Up

Jesus gave additional insight into His story about the Samaritan helping a Jew in His teaching in the Sermon on Mount: "You have heard that it was said, 'Love your neighbor and hate your enemy.' But I tell you, love your enemies" (Matthew 5:43 and 44). To the Pharisees "neighbor" referred only to fellow Jews, to those who were like them. And that is what led to the development of the wrong teaching that you were to hate your enemies—those not like you. Note how Jesus continued in Matthew 5:44-48. He says it is only natural to love those who love you and are like you. That's how the world lives. But Jesus calls His followers to be different from the world--we are to be like God, to show love to all, even those who don't love us.

How are we to love our neighbors? The Bible's answer is to love them as we love ourselves. To love our neighbor means we care about them and for them. We cannot love our neighbor in the abstract—we should note their need and try to meet it if we can. The Samaritan provides an example for us. I have a little book about the Gospel of Luke I purchased when I first started preaching in 1975. The author suggests four things we see in the Samaritan we need to cultivate to love our neighbor: vision to really see our neighbor, courage to act, flexibility in our schedule, and persistence to follow through.[10] I'm grateful the expert in the law asked Jesus the question, "Who is my neighbor?" Aren't you?

QUESTIONS FOR REFLECTION AND/OR DISCUSSION

1. How would you answer the question, "What must I do to inherit eternal life?"

2. What do you think was behind the question, "Who is my neighbor?" Was the expert still trying to "test" Jesus?

3. Can you imagine how those who first heard Jesus' story must have felt when it was a Samaritan who helped the man who had been beaten and robbed?

4. Is there any limitation today regarding who is our neighbor? Is there any limitation on what we might be expected to do to help our neighbor?

5. What do you think I mean in the closing paragraph that it takes vision to see and courage to act to help our neighbor?

6. Have you ever been in the position of the man who was in need and been helped by a neighbor?

CHAPTER NINE

"When Is Divorce Permissible?"

Primary Bible References – Matthew 19:1-12 and Mark 10:1-12

Several of the questions people asked Jesus are still relevant today, but none perhaps as much as the one about divorce. Divorce is quite acceptable in our contemporary society, but the question of when divorce is permissible is still discussed by those who are committed to the Lord and His Word.

Weddings are always exciting for those involved. Getting married is a life-changing occasion, but the wedding only marks the beginning. It's the marriage that follows the wedding–and the possibility of that marriage ending—that are the subject of this chapter's question to Jesus.

Context and Setting

Both Matthew and Mark record this incident, but the reports are not exactly the same. In what follows some attention will be given to the differences. This exchange with the Pharisees was not the only time Jesus discussed marriage and divorce. There is a brief teaching in the Sermon on the Mount in Matthew 5:21-22 and another in Luke 16:18, neither of which was prompted by a question.

The exchange about divorce took place as Jesus and His disciples traveled from Galilee in the north to Judea in the south. Matthew says, "Large crowds followed him, and He healed them there" (19:2) while Mark notes "crowds of people came to him, and as was his custom, he taught them" (10:1). It was typical of Jesus' ministry that He both healed and taught and He did so as He made His way to Jerusalem for the last time. What was also typical, in the midst of His teaching and healing, was that some Pharisees came to test Him.

Questioning Jesus and Considering His Responses

Both Matthew and Mark tell us the Pharisees came to test Jesus, but Matthew's account of their question has an additional phrase Mark's does not. Mark reports they asked Him, "Is it lawful for a man to divorce his wife?" (verse 2). Matthew, however, reports they asked Him, "Is it lawful for a man to divorce his wife for any and every reason?" (verse 3). While the questions are not exactly the same, they both do reflect the culture of the time with regard to men and women: divorce was an option only for men. In Judaism a wife did not have that option.

The additional phrase in Matthew's record, "for any and every reason," reflects Old Testament teaching and rabbinic interpretation of it that is not immediately obvious to us when we simply read it today. The question reflected the controversy of the time surrounding the interpretation of the teaching about divorce in Deuteronomy 24:1. The New International Version renders Deuteronomy 24:1 as follows: "If a man marries a woman who becomes displeasing to him because he finds something indecent about her, and writes her a certificate of divorce . . . ."

70

The question that was debated was the meaning of "something indecent about her." The two main schools of interpretation were from two rabbis (Shammai and Hillel) who represented a strict position and a lenient position. The lenient position was represented by the phrase "for any and every reason." (The example often cited for this position is that if the wife was a bad cook she could be divorced!) The strict position limited permissible divorce to some kind of sexual infidelity by the wife. The Pharisees were drawing Jesus into the dispute about the interpretation of the phrase and hoping that perhaps He would give an answer that contradicted the Mosaic Law.

Note first in Jesus' response in Matthew how He did not directly answer the question, but went all the way back to the Genesis account of the creation of male and female and the establishment of marriage. Jesus reminded His questioners that Genesis teaches "at the beginning the Creator made them male and female." And in marriage a man "is united to his wife, and they become one flesh." Jesus then adds His own observation that because of that, "what God has joined together, let no one separate" (Matthew 19:6). With His first response, Jesus seems to be suggesting there is no lawful reason for a man to divorce his wife.

The Pharisees responded to Jesus' answer by asking Him about a key provision in the Law about divorce in Deuteronomy 24:1-4. They paraphrased, "Why then did Moses command that a man give his wife a certificate of divorce and send her away?" (Matthew 19:7). There was indeed teaching in the Old Testament about divorce, but the Pharisees cited only the first part of it in order to press Jesus. The entire passage teaches that if a woman is divorced, remarries, and then divorces again, she cannot return to her first husband.

Jesus, of course, knew what Deuteronomy 24 said and was not surprised by their follow-up question. He replied, "Moses permitted you to divorce your wives because your hearts were hard. But it was not this way from the beginning" (verse 8). Note how Jesus changed their word "command" from Moses to "permitted" and again pointed them back to what He had already stated from Genesis. The "certificate of divorce" was a legal document indicating the dissolution of the marriage that allowed the woman to remarry. It was for her protection.

After Jesus' response regarding the "certificate of divorce" question He returned to their original question and in verse 9 answered it: "I tell you that anyone who divorces his wife, except for sexual immorality, and marries another woman commits adultery." Jesus took the strict position of only allowing divorce in the case of sexual unfaithfulness. While there is no unanimity among scholars concerning the exact meaning of the Greek word translated "sexual immorality," I agree with John Stott and others who suggest it points to behavior that in itself destroys the "one flesh" covenant reality of marriage.[11]

Something still needs to be said about this parallel account and why Mark does not have "the exception clause" from Jesus included in Matthew 19:9. I confess I don't have an answer; nor do I find any of a variety of proposals that have been put forth totally satisfying. If pressed on the matter, I would agree with the observation of some scholars that everyone at the time agreed sexual unfaithfulness was just cause for divorce and Mark took it for granted his readers knew that.[12]

Wrap Up

In dealing with divorce today I think Christians should follow the example Jesus set in His responses to the Pharisees. Before divorce is discussed we should first make sure we give attention to the meaning and purpose of marriage. Jesus did that by going back to the creation account of the institution of marriage. In contrast to so much thinking today, marriage is not a contract, but a covenant. After the marriage ceremony "they are no longer two, but one flesh." Therefore, God's original intent for marriage was and still is that it be life-long.

In addition to the divine ideal there is also the reality of human failure. God's ideal is not always carried out. And that is what is at the root of the Deuteronomy 24 passage, however it is interpreted. Jesus was clear that God permitted divorce because their "hearts were hard." Because of the reality of human failure marriages fail and divorces take place. The dissolution of a marriage may be the lesser of two evils, but the divine concession does not cancel the divine intention for marriage. Divorce is always a departure from God's ideal and can never be taken lightly.

Permission for divorce was granted because "sexual unfaithfulness" violated the "one flesh" unity and foundation of marriage. But just because divorce was permissible under such circumstances, it is not mandatory. In fact, most readers probably know couples who have experienced unfaithfulness in their marriage, but worked through it and rebuilt a stronger "one flesh" partnership than they had prior to the breach.

In this chapter I have not attempted to answer all the questions Christians ask about divorce and remarriage. That is not the purpose of this book and such a discussion would require an entire book. (Many books have been written about the issue!) I have tried to emphasize what Jesus emphasized in His response to the Pharisees' attempt to trap Him. We have to understand that according to Jesus, in God's eyes marriage is a permanent covenant commitment, and we need to hold high God's divine ideal.

Thankfully, neither adultery nor divorce are unforgiveable. In the same way that we hold God's divine ideal for marriage high, we also need to hold high the grace, love, and forgiveness of God. In terms of marriage and divorce my best suggestion is to begin with people where they are and go from there.

QUESTIONS FOR REFLECTION AND DISCUSSION

1. If you (or those in your group) are married, think back to your wedding day and try to remember what you were thinking, feeling and dreaming about your marriage on that day.

2. What kind of feelings did you have when you read in this chapter that divorce was once an option only for men, not for women?

3. How does today's reason of incompatibility or irreconcilable differences stand up to the Bible's teaching about divorce?

4. What is it about sexual immorality (by husband or wife) that tears so deeply at a marriage?

5. Look at Proverbs 6:27-35 and relate it to the subject of this chapter.

6. What are the keys to a long and fulfilling marriage?

CHAPTER TEN

"Who Do You Think You Are?"

Primary Bible References – Matthew 21:23-27; Mark 11:27-33; and Luke 20:1-8

One of the ways we might call someone down when we think they are out of line is to ask them, "Who do you think you are?" Parents sometimes ask that of their children. A teacher may ask that of a student. A supervisor might ask it of a subordinate. It's clearly not a question seeking information, but an expression of disagreement with something said or done. More than that, however, it is an attempt to put someone in his or her place. While the wording was a little different, a group of Jesus' critics used a similar question for the same reason.

Context and Setting

The questioning of Jesus we'll explore in this chapter took place during the final week of Jesus' life leading up to His crucifixion. It was the week of Passover and the roads were crowded with people going to Jerusalem. On Palm Sunday Jesus entered the city riding on a donkey with crowds cheering and spreading their cloaks and palm branches before Him. It resembled the entrance of a king and must have reminded some of the messianic prophecy of Zechariah 9:9: "Rejoice greatly, Daughter of Zion! Shout, Daughter of Jerusalem! See, your king comes to you righteous and victorious, lowly and riding on a donkey, on a colt, the foal of a donkey." Certainly Jesus' enemies noticed.

Then early in the week Jesus entered the temple and turned over the tables of the money-changers quoting Jeremiah 7:11, "It is written, 'My house will be called a house of prayer,' but you have made it 'a den of robbers'" (Matthew 21:13). This action also got everyone's attention, including His critics—who were not at all pleased.

Only Matthew reports that after this Jesus healed some who were blind and some who were lame. "But when the chief priests and the teachers of the law saw the wonderful things he did and the children shouting in the temple courts, 'Hosanna to the Son of David,' they were indignant" (Matthew 21:13). Matthew doesn't record it, but this must have been "the final straw" because Mark tells us that after the money-changers episode, "The chief priests and the teachers of the law heard this and began looking for a way to kill him, for they feared him, because the whole crowd was amazed at this teaching" (11:18).

Questioning Jesus

Jesus continued to teach every day in the temple. The questioning to be discussed in this chapter is the first of three that Jesus faced during that last week. (The next two chapters deal with the other two.) Matthew, Mark, and Luke all include this incident with only minor differences.

Mark tells us the chief priests, the teachers of the law, and the elders came to Jesus in the temple and demanded of Him, "By what authority are you doing these things? And who gave you authority to do this?" (11:27 and 28). This is the first time in these studies we have seen "the elders of the people" (Matthew 21:23) involved. They were local leaders and appear regularly from this point forward. One of the things they had to be referring to by "these things" was Jesus throwing out the money-changers, but they were also no doubt going back to the way He had entered the city on Palm Sunday and everything else He had done since then.

The chief priests, teachers of the law, and elders asked Jesus two related questions. They wanted to know what authority He had, and they wanted to know who gave it to Him. In other words, as suggested above, "Who do you think you are?" This questioning was similar to their request for a sign we looked at in chapter seven. They knew that to do what He was doing required some kind of authorization, and they knew they hadn't given Him that authority.

From these Gospel accounts, it's not immediately obvious what was behind this line of questioning. Perhaps they thought Jesus would claim the authority of the Messiah. He had certainly done and said things that suggested He thought He was the Messiah. But if He made that claim overtly the question was still relevant: who gave Him that authority? Not only that, they might accuse Him of blasphemy as they did a few days later when He was before the Sanhedrin.

Considering Jesus' Response

Throughout His ministry Jesus had taught and acted in His own name and with God's authority. That's why His disciples followed

Him and crowds came to hear Him. As a teacher Jesus was not like the other "official" teachers of the time. After Jesus preached the Sermon on the Mount, Matthew tells us "the crowds were amazed at his teaching, because he taught as one who had authority, and not as their teachers of the law" (7:28b and 29).

As we have seen throughout these studies, Jesus' response was masterful. At this point He was not yet ready to directly tell them He was the Son of God, so He responded with a question for them. "Answer me, and I will tell you by what authority I am doing these things. John's baptism—was it from heaven, or of human origin? Tell me!" (Mark 12:29 and 30). On first reading, Jesus' response seems evasive, but it really wasn't. It was the same basic question they had asked of Him, but Jesus' question was not about Himself, but John.

Jesus' question of His questioners put them on the spot. All three accounts tell us they argued (Matthew and Mark) or discussed (Luke) with one another their two possible answers, neither of which worked for them. They had not accepted John's message so they said to themselves, "If we say, 'From heaven,' he will ask, 'Then why didn't you believe him?'" (Mark 11:31). But because of John's popularity they reasoned among themselves, "But if we say, 'Of human origin'—we are afraid of the people, for they all hold that John was a prophet'" (Matthew 21:26).

New Testament scholar Alan Cole suggests Jesus was not trying to trap them, but to give them the opportunity to admit they were wrong and acknowledge that both John and Jesus were legitimate.[13] But they resolved their dilemma by giving the only answer they thought they could: "We don't know" (Mark 11:33a). That answer, of course, did not help them, but it served to authenticate Jesus.

Note that Jesus did not deny He had authority, but responded, "Neither will I tell you by what authority I am doing these things" (Mark 11:33b). Many in the crowd that day, as well as Jesus' critics, knew He approved of John as a true prophet. And John had approved of Jesus as a prophet and much more. If John's authority came from heaven, then so did Jesus' authority. Commentator R.T. France affirms, "No one who heard Jesus' response could fail to understand the implied claim to continuity between his ministry and that of John, and therefore to a divine authority for it."[14] But in the way Jesus handled the exchange, those who questioned Him could not use it against Him.

Wrap Up

It is telling that these critics were unwilling to answer Jesus' question. Even though they thought they knew the answer, they pleaded ignorance. But their non-answer was an expression of fear; not fear of bodily harm, but fear that the people would lose respect for them and their position. Ironically, their unwillingness even to answer Jesus' question probably also resulted in loss of respect for them among those witnessing the exchange.

You and I know not only who Jesus thought He was, we know who He was and is. And we know where He got His authority. He was and is the Son of God. And hopefully we will not hesitate to say what our position is when we are asked.

81

QUESTIONS FOR REFLECTION AND DISCUSSION

1. Can you remember a time when your parents or someone in authority asked you, "Just who do you think you are?"

2. Look at Zechariah 9:9 and relate the prophecy to the account of Jesus' entry into Jerusalem on Palm Sunday.

3. What do you think was going on when Jesus turned over the money-changers' tables in the Temple? Why did Jesus do that?

4. Why do you think Jesus refrained from simply telling His questioners that He was the Son of God?

5. In light of Jesus' question about John the Baptist and their refusal to answer, would it be fair to call these leaders cowards?

6. In your life with your friends and family, or at school or at work, are you ever tempted to withhold your testimony about your faith out of fear for what others might think?

CHAPTER ELEVEN

"Should We Pay Taxes?"

Matthew 22:15-22; Mark 12:13-17; and Luke 20:20-26

The subject of taxes seems to be a perennial subject at all levels of politics, and most of the talk is about how high or how unfair taxes are. Reasonable people understand taxes are a necessity, but we still don't like to pay them. The subject of taxes came up during Jesus' ministry as well. As on other occasions, it was the Pharisees who questioned Him about the issue. This is the second of three controversies with the religious leaders in the city of Jerusalem during the final week of Jesus' life.

Context and Setting

The purpose of the questioning of Jesus in this episode is clearly stated in the introduction in each of the accounts. Matthew reports, "Then the Pharisees went out and laid plans to trap him in his words" (22:15). Mark tells us "they sent some of the Pharisees and Herodians to Jesus to catch him in his words" (12:13). Luke introduces the account, "Keeping a close watch on him, they sent spies, who pretended to be sincere" (20:20).

In terms of Mark's introduction, scholars are not sure of the exact identity or views of the Herodians. They are, however, confident they supported the Herodian rule and therefore the Romans.[15] The fact that they teamed up with the Pharisees shows the animosity both groups had for Jesus. Today it would be similar to right-wing Republicans and radically liberal Democrats uniting to discredit a common enemy.

Questioning Jesus

Clearly the question posed to Jesus was not about gaining information. They wanted Jesus to say something that would get Him arrested. The word "trap" used here referred to capturing an animal in a net.

The exchange begins in Matthew and Mark with flattery, substantiating Luke's report that they "pretended to be sincere." Mark's account is the more complimentary of the two: "Teacher, we know that you are a man of integrity. You aren't swayed by others, because you pay no attention to who they are; but you teach the way of God in accordance with the truth" (12:14). I think they were trying to disarm Jesus by appearing to be sincere truth seekers and catching Him off-guard.

Whether they believed what they said or not, I am in total agreement with their observation, aren't you? Jesus was a man of integrity; He did teach the way of God in accordance with the truth; and He wasn't swayed by people according to their status or power. That's part of the reason He was such a great teacher.

Having set the table, so to speak, next came their question: "Is it right to pay the imperial tax to Caesar or not?" (Matthew 22:17). A footnote in the New International Version gives more insight into the issue, explaining the imperial tax was "a special tax levied on subject peoples, not on Roman citizens." Because of their faith, this was an especially delicate subject for the Jewish people.

Asking whether it was right to pay taxes to Caesar had nothing to do with any local law, but rather with the law of God. The question concerned whether faithful Jews living in Judea with God alone as their king should or should not pay taxes to the Roman emperor Caesar. And it was a subject of theological debate.

Those setting the trap were confident Jesus would be in trouble no matter how He answered the question. They thought He had to say either "yes" or "no" and either way they had Him. Whatever He said, He would be in trouble.

If Jesus said it was wrong to pay taxes to Caesar they would report it to the Roman governor and He could be arrested and charged. If He said it was lawful to pay taxes to Caesar He would offend those who thought as God's people they should not have to. The people would think of Him as unpatriotic, He would be discredited in the eyes of many, and He would lose much of his following.

For any other Rabbi this would have been a real dilemma.

Considering Jesus' Response

Jesus hadn't been taken in by their flattery. Matthew 22:18 tells us He knew "their evil intent" and called them "hypocrites." He then asked them, "Why are you trying to trap me?" Of course He knew why they were trying to trap Him, but He wanted them to know He knew.

Instead of immediately answering the question, Jesus asked them to show Him a coin used for paying the tax (Matthew 22:19). They brought Him a Roman coin (a denarius) and He asked them, "Whose image is this? And whose inscription?" (Matthew 22:20). They gave the only answer they could and indicated it was Caesar's.

After asking these questions, Jesus gave them their answer. In light of the answer they had given about the image and inscription on the coin Jesus said, "So give back to Caesar what is Caesar's and to God what is God's" (Matthew 22: 21). Jesus did not limit His answer to the question He was asked; He more than answered it by indicating their responsibility was not only to Caesar but also to God. Assessing Jesus' answer one commentator notes, "It left no room for an accusation of disloyalty to Caesar, but also stressed loyalty to God."[16]

Matthew concludes, "When they heard this, they were amazed. So they left him and went away" (22:22). Luke reports, "And astonished by his answer, they became silent" (20:26b). They thought they had the perfect plan to trap Jesus, but it hadn't worked.

Wrap Up

Jesus' answer to this questioning is relevant today. Regardless of where we live, Christians always have a dual citizenship both here and in heaven, and we are not to neglect our responsibilities in either realm. It is a misnomer to ever think that because we are Christians we do not have any duties as citizens and members of our community at large. As a matter of fact, Christians who are not good citizens damage their witness. We have a responsibility to pay our taxes and submit to the laws of the land in which we live. The State must be respected and its directions complied with within its own proper sphere. The Apostle Paul makes that clear in Romans 13:1: "Let everyone be subject to the governing authorities, for there is no authority except that which God has established." Christians should be known as good citizens. We should vote and some Christians should run for political office at every level.

However, as children of God our more important citizenship is in heaven. We are to render unto Caesar what is Caesar's, but we are also to render unto God what is His. That includes giving out of our financial resources to honor God, but it includes far more. It is the continuing goal of the Christian life to discover and learn God's will and submit to it. That's what it means to call Jesus "Lord" and is something we will hopefully grow in until our citizenship is completely in heaven.

These two citizenships have sometimes come into conflict and no doubt will again in the future. There are examples of this in both the Old and New Testaments, the early years of Christianity, and throughout history. When the time comes when rendering unto Caesar infringes upon our rendering unto God, our priority is with God. But I would caution readers never to confuse something you do not like about government policy with something that goes against God. The counsel of evangelical leader John Stott makes sense: "We are to submit right up to the point where obedience to the state would entail disobedience to God. If the state commands what God forbids, or forbids what God commands, then our plain Christian duty is to resist, not to submit, to disobey the state in order to obey God."[17]

Jesus, a man of integrity who taught the way of God in accordance with truth and who wasn't swayed by people, still tells us today to dutifully pay our taxes to the government and generously give to God for His glory.

QUESTIONS FOR REFLECTION AND/OR DISCUSSION

1. What are your thoughts about the variety of taxes you pay? Do you think they are unfair or too high?

2. Why do you think the Pharisees teamed up with the Herodians in setting this trap for Jesus?

3. Can you remember a time in your life when you flattered someone with the goal of disarming them to get something from them? (A parent, a teacher, a boss, etc.)

4. What do you think in means in this chapter when I suggest "Christians who are not good citizens damage their witness?"

5. See Philippians 3:20. What does this idea of citizenship in heaven mean to you?

6. Can you imagine a time when your status as a citizen of heaven (a follower of Christ) may conflict with your citizenship where you now live? Do you know of situations where it is happening now? How do you think you would respond?

CHAPTER TWELVE

"Which Commandment Is at the Top of Your List?"

Primary Bible References – Matthew 22:34-40 and Mark 12:28-34

Choosing your favorite is not always easy, is it? If you have been blessed with two or more children, which is your favorite? I have two children. I tell Audrey she is my favorite daughter and I tell Rob he is my favorite son. If you love dogs and have had a series of them through the years, can you pick one as your favorite? Probably not. The questioning of Jesus we will look at in this chapter is about His view of the greatest commandment. Admittedly it is not about Jesus' favorite commandment, but you get the point. Perhaps we can say this discussion was about which commandment Jesus would have at the top of the list.

Context and Setting

Like many of the other incidents we have studied, the one in this chapter also involves the Pharisees (in Matthew's account) and a teacher of the law (in Mark's). But it follows immediately upon an exchange between Jesus and the Sadducees. The Sadducees were the other primary group of religious leaders talked about in the Gospels. Sociologically they were generally more aristocratic and wealthy than the Pharisees, and unlike the Pharisees, they were centered in Jerusalem. Therefore, the Sadducees were not popular among the masses like the Pharisees were.[18]

The Sadducees also differed doctrinally from the Pharisees. The Sadducees rejected the accumulated traditions of the Pharisees and did not believe in the resurrection of the dead as the Pharisees did. And yet we saw in chapter seven how both groups were united in questioning Jesus about a sign. Just before the story we're going to study in this chapter, the Sadducees had asked Jesus a question about resurrection and the afterlife. The ensuing dialogue is the final controversy with the religious leaders in Jerusalem during the final week of Jesus' life.

Questioning Jesus

Mark tells us one of the teachers of the law heard the exchange between the Sadducees and Jesus and noticed "that Jesus had given them a good answer" (Mark 12:28). Matthew reports the Pharisees heard "that Jesus had silenced the Sadducees" (Matthew 22:34). It was His good answer that silenced them.

Now it was the Pharisees' turn. Mark says it was "a teacher of the law," but Matthew notes it was "an expert in the law" who tested Jesus with a question. They were not seeking information. Matthew records the question: "Teacher, which is the greatest commandment in the Law?" (Matthew 22:36). Mark phrases it, "Of all the commandments, which is the most important?" (Mark 12:28).

Aside from trying to trap Jesus, it was an interesting question. If you're not familiar with Jesus' answer, I'm sure you want to know

what it was. Our thoughts probably go first to the Ten Commandments. Which is the most important or the greatest? But we should
remind ourselves there were many more commandments in the Law
than those ten. In fact, there were a total of 613 commandments; 365
negative and 248 positive. Of these 613, including the top ten, which
is the greatest?

In simply reading this question today it is not obvious how it was
intended as a "test" for Jesus. One New Testament scholar notes rabbis
at the time had such discussions, but they did not all agree. "Any answer must risk pleasing some at the expense of alienating others, and
therein perhaps is the element of 'test' from an unsympathetic dialogue partner."[19] The questioning in this case does not seem to be on
the level of the others we are examining, but Jesus' answer certainly
is.

Considering Jesus' Response

Jesus gave a masterful answer that went beyond the original question and put the entire Old Testament in perspective. Note Jesus' response as recorded by Matthew: "'Love the Lord your God with all
your heart and with all your soul and with all your mind.' This is the
first and greatest commandment. And the second is like it: 'Love your
neighbor as yourself.' All the Law and Prophets hang on these two
commandments" (verses 37-40).

Jesus taught that the first and greatest commandment is to completely love God. Interestingly enough, neither this first commandment nor Jesus' second greatest commandment are taken from the

Ten Commandments. Nevertheless, both are taken from the Old Testament Law; one from Deuteronomy 6:5 and the other from Leviticus 19:18.

On the surface Jesus' greatest commandment may seem too simple to us, but with a little more thought I think we will agree with Jesus. And consider what is not the greatest commandment: it is not worship God, it is not fear God, it is not obey God--it is love God. In all of being and living as a Christian, nothing is more important, and nothing substitutes for loving God. It is still the greatest commandment today.

In this commandment we are told how to love God—"with all your heart and with all your soul and with all your mind." When the Bible uses the word "heart" it generally isn't referring to the organ that pumps our blood, but rather the seat of emotions and of love in particular. To love God with all your heart rules out half-heartedness.

Loving God "with all our soul" points to the personal aspect of our relationship with God. Love of God is personal. He is a person and loving Him is an interpersonal relationship. His love of us is personal. He knows who we are, our name, and everything about us.

The third aspect of completely loving God in this passage is "with all your mind." That is especially interesting because Deuteronomy 6:5 says "with all your strength." I'm not sure why Jesus made the change, but I do think loving God with "our mind" speaks to loving Him with all our strength. While loving God with our hearts suggests emotion, we are not to love God just with emotion. Living the Christian faith includes loving God with both one's heart and one's head.

To love God completely does not mean we cannot love others at the same time. It does mean that no other person or thing can take the place of God in our lives—not our job, not our hobby, not our house, not our family, not even our church.

Even though Jesus wasn't asked, He went on to say the second greatest commandment is to "Love your neighbor as yourself." Some find the premise of this commandment, that you love yourself, troubling. Is it wrong to love yourself? Yes, and no. There is a kind of self-love that is wrong. It is a selfish, self-centered love that only cares about self. It is what the Apostle Paul is speaking of in II Timothy 3:2 when he writes, "People will be lovers of themselves." We all know people who are guilty of this wrong kind of self-love.

But there is a kind of self-love that is not wrong, that is not expressed through selfishness, that is good and needed. I can't imagine the Old Testament or Jesus would give a command that issues out of a wrong stance. An appropriate self-love comes from realizing who we are and how valuable we are to God.

It is this kind of self-love that informs this second greatest commandment. I suppose we might ask whether or not it is possible to command love. If we cannot legislate morality, can we command love? Probably not the kind of love that comes most often to our minds when we hear it; not the involuntary response of warmth and affection. I don't think it is possible for us to have that kind of love for everyone, and certainly not upon command.

When Jesus tells us to love our neighbor He doesn't mean that kind of love. The kind of love Jesus is talking about is intentional. It is love that acts in the best interest of the one loved. To obey the second greatest commandment, we need not worry about feeling love.

To love your neighbor as yourself reminds me of Jesus' well-known instruction, "Do to others as you would have them do to you" (Luke 6:31). (To explore who qualifies as one's neighbor and what it involves return to chapter eight.)

Jesus concluded His response, "All the Law and the Prophets hang on these two commandments." It's not hard to see why Jesus said loving God is the greatest commandment and loving your neighbor is the second greatest. In doing so He raised the discussion above competing rules to underscore the priority of love in all of life. According to Jesus, that is actually what the Law and the Prophets are all about.

Wrap Up

Mark's account includes an affirmation of Jesus from His questioner. He noted that the two commandments Jesus specified are "more important than all burnt offerings and sacrifice" (Mark 12:33). Love is supreme. To which Jesus declared, "You are not far from the kingdom of God" (verse 34). Mark then tells his readers, "And from then on no one dared ask him any more questions." That is true in terms of the kind of questions we have been examining so far; but Jesus was questioned after this by those who tried Him prior to His crucifixion.

QUESTIONS FOR REFLECTION AND/OR DISCUSSION

1. How do you think this question "tested" Jesus?

2. Do you think "love God completely" is a good paraphrase for "Love the Lord your God with all your heart and with all your soul and with all your mind?"

3. If you had to choose one, would you say you are more of a "heart Christian" or more of a "head Christian?" Why?

4. In Psalm 23:3 David says God "refreshes my soul." What does that mean and does God refresh your soul? How does one love God with his soul?

5. What is the difference between an appropriate love of oneself and an inappropriate love of oneself?

6. Can you really love someone (your neighbor) you don't like? Elaborate.

CHAPTER THIRTEEN

"Are You the King of the Jews?"

Primary Bible Reference – Matthew 27:11-14; Mark 15:2-5; Luke 23:2-5; and John 18:28-19:16

The most dramatic and consequential questioning of Jesus took place during the hearings and trials He went through prior to His crucifixion. Actors have tried to capture the drama in a multitude of plays and movies ranging from small church youth-led Good Friday services to the big screen of Hollywood.

But the consequences were more important than the drama. For Jesus it meant His death on the cross. Of course He knew the reason He came was to die, but His prayer in the Garden of Gethsemane gives us insight into His inner struggle. In addition, the consequence of His death was an opportunity for us to have life, through the forgiveness of our sin and restoration of our status as children of God.

Context and Setting

The accounts of the night of Jesus' arrest and trials, all the way through His resurrection and ascension, are in many respects the most difficult to harmonize in the Gospels. The trials before His crucifixion and His appearances after His resurrection are most challenging.

John's account of Jesus before Pilate is the most complete of the four with Matthew and Mark being in the most agreement about the entire ordeal. I suggest reading and studying one account at a time and not investing a great deal of time and energy in trying to harmonize everything.

In terms of the questioning of Jesus prior to His crucifixion, the questioning from Pilate was the final stage. Prior to appearing before Pilate Jesus went before Jewish authorities two or three times. It seems clear Jesus was first questioned informally and then later taken before the Sanhedrin (the formal Jewish council). Only John tells us that Jesus was taken first to Annas, the father-in-law of the high priest Caiaphas (18:13). After that He was taken "to Caiaphas the high priest, where the scribes and the elders had gathered" (Matthew 26:57).

Early the next morning the night's questionings came to a climax. This exchange is also the high point of all that had transpired between Jesus and His critics during His final week.

The Jewish leaders were looking for evidence to charge Jesus so they could put Him to death. In the first part of the "hearing" they couldn't get two witnesses to agree. Finally, two agreed about Jesus saying He was able to destroy the temple and rebuild it in three days. Yet even with the high priest challenging Him to respond, Jesus remained silent.

Finally, exasperated, the high priest challenged Him: "I charge you under oath by the living God: Tell us if you are the Messiah of God" (Matthew 26:63). By the things He had done and said, especially in recent days, Jesus had given enough reason for the high priest to ask the question. Matthew, Mark, and Luke all report Jesus' answer a little differently; Matthew has Him saying, "You have said so" (Matthew

26:64a). As we will see later, this is very similar to the response Jesus would soon give to Pilate.

But the answer that brought everything to a head was what Jesus said next: "But I say to all of you: From now on you will see the Son of Man sitting at the right hand of the Mighty One and coming on the clouds of heaven" (Matthew 26:64b). It was a bold statement claiming a special relationship with God no human being could have. The high priest tore his clothes (a sign that blasphemy had been committed) and said, "He has spoken blasphemy! Why do we need any more witnesses? Look, now you have heard the blasphemy. What do you think?" (Matthew 26:65 and 66a). And all agreed Jesus was worthy of death.

The final note of context and setting is Matthew 27:1 and 2: "Early in the morning, all the chief priests and the elders of the people made their plans how to have Jesus executed. So they bound him, led him away and handed him over to Pilate the governor."

Questioning Jesus and Considering His Responses

Since John's account of Jesus before Pilate gives the most detail, we will use it in this part of our study. Pilate began the proceedings by asking the Jewish leaders what charges they were bringing against Jesus (18:29). These enemies of Jesus knew they didn't have a charge that would stand up in the Roman court so their response was Jesus was a criminal. In the first of several efforts to remove himself from the situation, Pilate told them, "Take him yourselves and judge him by your own law" (18:31).

The leaders' response was they did not have the right to execute anyone; this was the very reason they had taken Jesus to Pilate. The Roman government did not permit its subjects to convict and carry out the death penalty. That was in the hands of the local governor. The leaders' problem was compounded in that blasphemy was a serious infraction for the Jews, but meant nothing to the Romans.

It was at this point that Pilate asked the key question. The question is identical in all four Gospels: "Are you the king of the Jews?" (Matthew 27:11; Mark 15:2; Luke 23:3; and John 18:33). The question is identical, but the recorded response of Jesus is not. Matthew, Mark, and Luke all have Jesus responding, "You have said so," the same response Jesus had given earlier to the high priest. R.T. France notes this answer "is a qualified affirmative," indicating yes to the question, but not in accordance with the meaning the questioner has in mind.[20] In other words, Jesus was agreeing He was indeed a king, but not in the way Pilate was using the word.

John's fuller account of the exchange between Jesus and Pilate bears out France's interpretation of Jesus' answer recorded in the other Gospels. John tells us Jesus' responded with a question: "Is that your own idea, or did others talk to you about me?" (18:34). It seems pretty clear that Jesus' accusers had set Him up ahead of time. Pilate responded, "Am I a Jew? Your own people and chief priests handed you over to me. What is it you have done?" (18:35)

The final part of Jesus' response to Pilate is one of His best-known sayings: "My kingdom is not of this world. If it were, my servants would fight to prevent my arrest by the Jewish leaders. But now my kingdom is from another place" (18:36). He had a kingdom, but it was not like the world's kingdoms. If it was His disciples would have fought for Him.

Only Luke tells us that at this point in the proceedings Pilate learned Jesus was from Galilee and sent Him to Herod (Luke 26:6:12). This was the second attempt by Pilate to opt out of dealing with Jesus. But Herod sent Him back to Pilate.

Pilate made two more attempts to get out of dealing with the charges and requests the Jewish leaders brought to him about Jesus. He brought up the custom of releasing a prisoner at the time of Passover and offered to release "the king of the Jews" (John 18:39). Instead they chose Barabbas. Pilate also repeated his view that Jesus was innocent by declaring, "I find no basis for a charge against him" (John 19:6b).

In John's account Pilate also continued questioning Jesus, concluding with, "Don't you realize I have power either to free you or to crucify you?" (19:10). In Jesus' final words to Pilate He gave another bold and powerful answer: "You would have no power over me if it were not given to you from above. Therefore, the one who handed me over to you is guilty of a greater sin" (19:11). Jesus told Pilate the only power he had over Him was given to him by God. And even though Caiaphas (probably) was guiltier, Pilate was also guilty.

Wrap Up

Pilate was a conflicted leader who tried hard, but not hard enough. John tells us, "From then on Pilate tried to set Jesus free" (19:12a). But the Jewish leaders would not accept it. The final straw for Pilate was no doubt what these leaders had in mind when they first took Jesus to him. They told Pilate, "If you let this man go, you are no friend of Caesar. Anyone who claims to be a king opposes Caesar" (19:12b).

Even though I have known the account since I was child, and have heard it more times than I can count, I think one of the saddest verses in the Bible is John 19:16: "Finally Pilate handed him to them to be crucified."

QUESTIONS FOR REFLECTION AND/OR DISCUSSION

1. Why did the Jewish leaders want to have Jesus executed?

2. Exactly what was Jesus claiming with His words in Matthew 26:64b?

3. What is Jesus' kingdom and how is it different from kingdoms of this world?

4. What kind of man was Pilate? (Note how he tried to get out of executing Jesus.)

5. Did you see Mel Gibson's film The Passion of the Christ? What do you remember about it and how did it impact you?

6. Reflect on what Jesus' followers must have felt and imagine what they talked about following Jesus' crucifixion.

CONCLUSION

Sometimes after a friend has introduced us to someone he really wanted us to meet, the friend will ask, "Well, what did you think?" Our friend already has an appreciation for whomever they have introduced to us, but he wants to know what we think about that person. Are we impressed? Do we like the person? Do we approve?

Now that you've explored these different accounts of Jesus being questioned and considered His responses, what do you think? If you knew a lot about Jesus before you read these reflections, I'm pretty sure you already liked and appreciated Him. If that is the case, I hope you are even fonder of Him and more impressed by Him.

If you didn't know much about Jesus before reading these reports from the Bible, what do you think? Are you impressed? Do you like Him? Do you approve? Did He do or say anything in these accounts that got your attention and drew you to Him?

The reason I wrote this book about these particular selections from the records of Jesus' life and ministry was to help readers get to know Him better, both those who came to the book with little knowledge of the Gospels as well as those who already knew a great deal about them. I've been reading and talking about all of this at a variety of levels for over 50 years, but after focusing on these 13 incidents I am more impressed by Jesus and know Him better than I ever have.

Jesus was the greatest teacher who ever lived, and as a teacher He had immeasurable impact upon those He taught. Even Jesus' critics responded with amazement to his teachings—remember chapter 11 and their questioning about taxes? Various translations say the Pharisees were amazed, that they marveled, that they were astonished and speechless. Even when it wasn't recorded in the other accounts, I think those who heard Jesus' responses were amazed, and we are still amazed today when we hear what He said.

Who was this Jesus who was questioned and gave these amazing responses? In light of what He said, it is pretty clear who Jesus thought He was. And in the rest of the New Testament it is clear who His first and early followers thought He was. If we are amazed at His teachings, it makes sense for us to consider what Jesus and His followers said. In concluding these studies I want to underscore two passages from two of the Gospel accounts.

The first is from Jesus Himself following His death, burial, and resurrection and before His ascension to heaven. Matthew 28:18-20 tells us His final words to His disciples were, "All authority in heaven and earth has been given to me. Therefore go and make disciples of all nations, baptizing them in the name of the Father and of the Son and of the Holy Spirit, and teaching them to obey everything I have commanded you. And surely I am with you always, to the very end of the age."

Jesus makes the powerful claim that all authority has been given to Him. And based upon that, those who would become His followers are to be taught to obey everything He had commanded. He then promises that He will always be with them. There can be little doubt who Jesus thought He was.

The second passage is from the end of the Gospel of John before the final chapter, often called the appendix. John 20:30 and 31 tells us, "Jesus performed many other signs in the presence of his disciples, which are not recorded in this book. But these are written that you may believe that Jesus is the Messiah, the Son of God, and that by believing you may have life in his name."

John tells his readers the purpose of his writing is that they would come to believe something about Jesus—that He was the Messiah, the Son of God. Both designations indicate who Jesus was and is. To believe in Him is to have life. There can be little doubt who this writer thought Jesus was.

In the introduction to this book we noted Christology is the study of who Jesus was and what He did. But it is much more than that. For those who are His disciples today it is also about who Jesus still is and what He still does. We are still amazed and impressed by Him. But more than that, we place our faith in Him as our Savior and commit to follow Him as our Lord.

NOTES

Introduction

1. Lee Strobel has written two excellent books that deal with apologetics. The Case for Christ (Grand Rapids: Zondervan Publishing House, 1998) deals with objections and questions about Jesus and the biblical records. The Case for Faith (Grand Rapids: Zondervan, 2000) deals with the broader and more philosophical objections to Christianity.

Chapter 1

2. Bruce M. Metzger, The New Testament: Its Background, Growth, and Content (Nashville: Abingdon, 1965) 111.

Chapter 3

3. Leon Morris, The Gospel According to St. Luke (Grand Rapids: William B. Eerdmans, 1974) 119.
4. Arron Chambers, Eats with Sinners: Reaching Hungry People Like Jesus Did (Cincinnati: Standard Publishing, 2009) 10.

Chapter 4

5. A book I recommend that deals with this issue is Mark D. Roberts' Can We Trust the Gospels: Investigating the Reliability of Matthew, Mark, Luke, and John (Wheaton: Crossway Books, 2007).

Chapter 6

6. Leon Morris, Reflections on the Gospel of John (Peabody: Hendrickson Publishers, 2000) 291.

Chapter 7

7. Leon Morris, The Gospel According to John (Grand Rapids: William B. Eerdmans, 1975) 197.

8. Alan Cole, The Gospels According to Mark (Grand Rapids: William B. Eerdmans, 1973) 128.

9. A helpful discussion of this incident and application for today can be found in J.I. Packer, Guard Us, Guide Us: Divine Leading in Life's Decisions (Grand Rapids: Baker Books, 2008) pp. 39-44.

Chapter 8

10. William C. Brownson, Jr., Distinctive Lessons from Luke (Grand Rapids: Baker Book House, 1974) pp. 54-58.

Chapter 9

11. John R.W. Stott, Divorce (Downers Grove: InterVarsity Press, 1973) 20.

12. R.T. France, The Gospel of Matthew (Grand Rapids: Wm. B. Eerdmans Publishing Co., 2007) 211. See also Stott, Divorce, 17.

Chapter 10

13. Cole, The Gospel According to St. Mark, 183.

14. France, The Gospel of Matthew, 799.

Chapter 11

15. Metzger, The New Testament: Its Background, Growth, and Content, 44.

16. Morris, The Gospel According to St. Luke, 289.

17. John Stott, Romans: God's Good New for the World (Downers Grove, InterVarsity Press, 1994) 342 and 343.

Chapter 12

18. Metzger, The New Testament: Its Background, Growth, and Content, 43.

19. France, The Gospel of Matthew, 842.

Chapter 13

20. France, The Gospel of Matthew, 1026.

ABOUT THE AUTHOR

Bob Mink served as summer youth minister and youth minister in churches in Ohio, as minister of a small church in Pennsylvania, and as pastor of a large church in Southern California. A graduate of Cincinnati Christian University, Bob also has a Master of Divinity and a Doctor of Ministry from Eastern Baptist Theological Seminary, a Master of Theology from Princeton Theological Seminary, and a Master of Arts in Religion from Temple University. He currently is Adjunct Professor of Biblical Studies at Hope International University in Fullerton, California and the author of A Pastor and the People: An Inside Look through Letters. Bob can be contacted by email at bobmmink@gmail.com.

Made in the USA
San Bernardino, CA
18 February 2016